Ribbon Bars
&
Knot Awards
of the
Boy Scouts of America

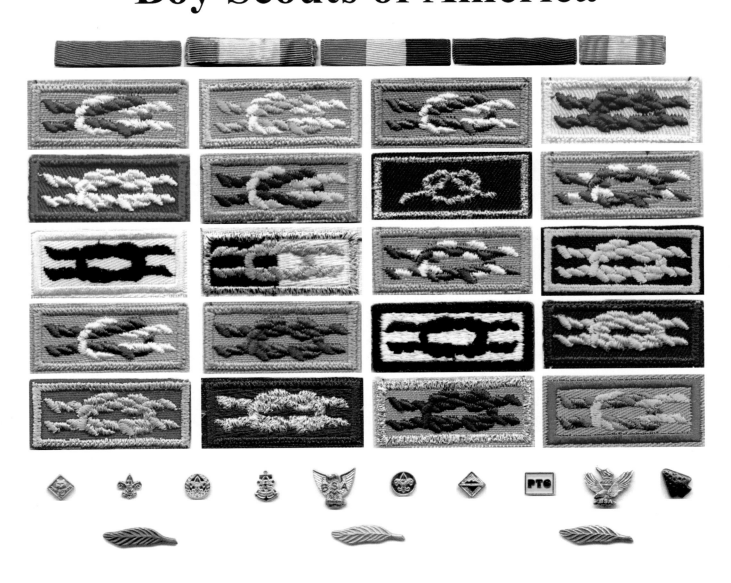

Gary E. Whitman

7th Edition

Published by 1903 press
www.1903.com
Fishers, IN
United States of America

ii

Preface

I compiled this book to provide information on all ribbon bars, knot awards, devices, and eagle palms that have been issued by the Boy Scouts of America. This includes what the knot was issued for and what it represents. It is also helpful to know the requirements for the various knots so that one understands the effort and time of involvement and the commitment a Scouter has invested to earn the recognition. Scouts notice when their leaders wear knot awards. It is important for leaders to wear their knot awards to show their levels of achievement and training.

I have included a chapter with a comprehensive listing of knot awards (K-List) showing all known varieties of every knot. In addition similar lists are provided of all devices (D-List), and Eagle Palms (EP-List). In the development of the K-List in this version I was greatly assisted by George Crowl. In previous editions I had assistance from Shay Lelegren, Arnold Traupman, and Bruce Noonan.

The List of Devices (D-List) depicts all changes to the devices. The D-List was developed with assistance from George Crowl and special help from Dr. Terry Grove on the Distinguished Eagle devices. Dr. Grove also helped on the section on Eagle Palms.

Prior to 1980 there was a prescribed order of precedence for the wearing of knot awards. The most prestigious knot was positioned to the top inside (wearer's right). Over the years the order of precedence changed. I have provided information on these changes.

Special thanks go to George Crowl, Dr. Terry Grove, Mitch Reis, Shay Lelegren, Arnold Traupman, Joe Weingarten, and Hal Yocum for their assistance in the development of this book. George, Shay, and Arnold assisted in the development of the K-List. George assisted in the development of the Listing of Knot Awards and the Listing of Devices. Terry assisted with the Listing of Eagle. George and Mitch provided scans of some ribbon bars. Hal was responsible for my including the Ribbon Bars and K-List in the book. Joe edited this book and converted the format for publication.

A book of this nature in many cases may miss a knot award, device, or eagle palm and is always in revision as more information is found. If you have additional information or have a question please get in touch with me. I have listed my address, phone number and e-mail below. I plan on periodically updated to include changes in the requirements and additional knots that may be added or changed by the Boy Scouts of America.

> Gary E. Whitman
> 5401 S. FM1626, Suite 170-242
> Kyle, Texas 78640
> 512-636-2109
> e-mail: TxHazMatMan@prodigy.net

Note: If you send me an e-mail, use "BSA Knots" as the subject line. My preferred method of communication is telephone.

Yours in Scouting,

Gary E. Whitman

Gary E. Whitman

Table of Contents / Index

Devices for Knot Awards (Listed Alphabetically)

History

In 1934, the Boy Scouts of America issued ribbon bars for wear on Scouter's (adults) Boy Scout uniform to signify the recipient had received an award. These bars were not to be worn during formal ceremonies. The awards that were recognized were the Honor Medal, Silver Buffalo, Silver Beaver, Eagle Scout, Quartermaster, Scoutmaster's Key, and Scouter's Training Award. When the Silver Antelope was first awarded in 1944 an additional ribbon bar was produced for that award. There were also contest medals produced prior to that time period resembling ribbon bar awards. Those bars had a crude hook instead of a spin latch clasp. The ribbon bars appeared to look and were worn like military decorations. All publications show that in 1941 the length of the Scoutmaster's Key and Scouter's Training Award ribbon were shortened to 7/8". It is believed that it was a misprint for the earlier years for these 2 ribbon bars, as the publications all say that the bar contained a portion of the actual ribbon. The ribbon was never the length originally stated for these 2 bars. In 1942 the Eagle Scout bar was widened to 7/16" and a miniature eagle pin was added to the center of the bar.

It was announced in January (1946) Scouting Magazine: *"Wearing of ribbon bar pins indicating Scout honors or awards has been suspended to avoid confusion with military ribbons, and that a new method of indicating Scout honors would be provided for use on the uniform. A new insignia has been created to replace the bar pins formally used to represent Scouter awards. It consists of a square knot, embroidered on khaki cloth and is worn above the left breast pocket... The use of the cloth insignia is optional and the medal badge may be worn as desired. The special awards and their identifying colored knots are as follows: Silver Buffalo – red and white, Silver Antelope – orange and white, Silver Beaver – light blue and white, Scoutmaster's key – green and white, and Scouter's Training Award – green. No insignia is provided to replace the bar pin previously used to represent the Eagle rank, because embroidered insignia is available for this purpose. The use of all ribbon bar pins will be discontinued[1]."*

As late as January 1947 the Eagle Scout ribbon bar was the only one still offered for sale[2]. In October 1947[3], there were 9 knots available for sale. In addition to the 5 knots announced in March 1946, knots for Eagle Scout, Quartermaster, Honor Medal, and Skipper's Key were added.

Over the years, additional knots were introduced. Knots have been produced with a variety of twill/weave designs and backings. It is not the intent of this author to show every twill design/backing that has been produced. The intent is to show the various knots, to include the primary background and border color changes that have taken place during the years and to show the requirements for the earned knot recognitions.

Knots are worn with the distinguishing color to the wearer's right [example; Silver Beaver, page 9, has blue rope to the wearers right (left as you are looking at it)]. All knots have the "over loop" of the square knot to the wearer's right. When white is part of the knot, it is always the non-dominant color, and to the wearer's left (right as you are looking at it).

Councils have issued unauthorized knots over the years. The Boy Scouts of America did not approve those council issues. As published in *Prospeak* (the Scouting professional magazine), Volume 19, Number 2, February 2005, page 9, *"Local councils cannot issue and approve uniform knots. The insignia and uniform committee of the BSA is always a part of the approval process at the National Council.* It also stated: *No alteration of, or additions to, the official uniforms, as described in the official publications, or the rules and regulations covering the wearing of the uniform and the proper combinations thereof on official occasions, may be authorized by any Scouting official or local council*

---

[1] Published in the March Scouting magazine – 1946, page 27
[2] January 1, 1947 Price List of Official Uniforms and Equipment
[3] Information listed in *The Scout Executive* Vol. 12, No. 7.

or any local executive board or committee, except the Executive Board of the Boy Scouts of America after consideration by the Program Group Committee."

All knots issued by the Boy Scouts of America are pictured in this book. Knot recognition includes what the knot was issued for and what it represents. It is also helpful to know the requirements for the various knots so that one understands the effort and time of involvement and the commitment a Scouter might have invested to earn the recognition.

Prior to 1980 there was a prescribed order of precedence for the wearing of knot awards. The most prestigious knot was positioned to the top inside (wearer's right). Over the years the order of precedence changed.

The following index of awards provides the key for the knots awards used up to 1980.

Index of awards

AA	Air Ace Award	RA	Ranger
AOL	Arrow of Light	RE	Religious Emblem
DAM	District Award of Merit	REA	Religious Emblem - Adult
DLC	Den Leader Coach's Training Award	REY	Religious Emblem – Youth
DLT	Den Leader's Training Award	SA	Silver Antelope Award
DSA	OA Distinguished Service Award	SB	Silver Beaver Award
E	Eagle Scout Award	SBuf	Silver Buffalo Award
ESA	Explorer Silver Award	SK	Scouter's Key
HM	Honor Medal	SSSK	Skipper's Key (Sea Scout) - Discontinued
MM	Medal of Merit		1948
OSO	Knots from other scouting organizations	STA	Scouter's Training Award
QM	Quartermaster	SW	Silver World

The following graph contains a history of the published order of precedence for the wear of knot awards:

Order of Precedence

Order	1953	1954	1956[4]	1966	1969	1973	1977[5]	1978	1979
1	HM	HM	HM	HM	HM	HM	HM	HM	HM
2	SBuf	SBuf	SBuf	SBuf	SBuf	SBuf	SW	SW	SW
3	SA	SA	SA	SA	SA	SA	SBuf	SBuf	SBuf
4	SB	SB	SB	SB	SB	SB	SA	SA	SA
5	MM	MM	MM	MM	MM	MM	SB	SB	SB
6	E	E	E	E	E	E	MM	DAM	DAM
7	QM *	QM *	QM *	QM	QM	QM	E	DSA	DSA
8	AA *	AA *	ESA *	ESA	ESA	RE	QM *	MM	MM
9	ESA *	ESA *	FSD	SK or STA[6]	SK	OSO	RA / ESA[7]*	E	AOL[8]

---

[4] No more than 5 embroidered square knots may be worn at one time
[5] Knots are worn in rows of 3 above the left pocket. There is no limit to the number of knots that can be worn, if earned. Only one Scouter's Key and/or Scouter's Training Award knot may be worn. Device(s) is/are added to depict which program(s) the Scouter's Key and/or Scouter's Training award was earned.
[6] Same knot – only Scouter's Key has devices
[7] Ranger or either Silver Award

Order	1953	1954	1956[9]	1966	1969	1973	1977[10]	1978	1979
10	SK or STA[11]	OSO[12]	OSO		STA	SK	REY	QM	E
11		SK or STA[13]	SK[14]			STA[15]	REA	ESA[16]	QM
12						DAM	OSO[17]	REY[18]	ESA
13							SK	REA	REY
14							STA	OSO	REA
15							DLT	SK	OSO
16							DLC	STA	SK
17							DAM	DLT	STA
18							DSA	DLC	DLT
19									DLC

* Worn in order earned

Note: The above list depict knots current as of the publication dates of the appropriate Boy Scouts of America manuals from 1953 to 1979. All knot awards that were created after 1979 are not listed, as the order of precedence, for the wear of knot awards, was no longer in effect.

The Arrow of Light knot was announced in the October 1979 edition of the Scouter's Magazine. This announcement placed the Arrow of Light higher in the order of precedence than the Eagle Scout award. The BSA National Office received approximately one million letters of complaint over this issue. As a result, starting in 1980, the order for wearing knot awards was based on the important of the wearer.

It was important to include the devices used on knots. The majority of the devices have had minor changes in design appearance resulting from changes in manufacturers. The minor differences are difficult to detect without studying the various devices. The basic design however has remained the same. The earlier devices were manufactured with better detail. They also had a short attachment pin, which made it difficult to attach to a knot. In 1969 the attachment pin was lengthened to accommodate the thickness of the knot. Due to the size of the devices, it is very difficult to distinguish the minor differences, especially in a photograph. With two exceptions, only one scan of each device has been included in this book. Both the commissioner and Distinguished Eagle Scout devices have had a major change in style, therefore the main style differences for both of these devices are included.

Eagle palms were first introduced in 1926. There have only been two basic styles of the Bronze, Gold and Silver palms. There are a number of listed types for the second style, however all of those types are minor variations.

---

[8] The October 1979 edition of the Scouter's Magazine announced the newly created Arrow of Light square knot. The order of precedence was still in existence and placed the location at the 9th position, between the Medal of Merit and Eagle Scout award.
[9] No more than 5 embroidered square knots may be worn at one time
[10] Knots are worn in rows of 3 above the left pocket. There is no limit to the number of knots that can be worn, if earned. Only one Scouter's Key and/or Scouter's Training Award knot may be worn. Device(s) is/are added to depict which program(s) the Scouter's Key and/or Scouter's Training award was earned.
[11] Only one may be worn
[12] Termed Foreign Scout Decorations, in 1973 the term Foreign Scout Decorations was used, and in 1977 Awards from Scout associations of other nations if knot is awarded is the way it was listed.
[13] Only one may be worn
[14] Represents Scouter's Key and Scouter's Training Award
[15] Starting in 1975 devices are authorized on the Scouter's Training Award
[16] Also includes Ranger & Air Explorer Ace
[17] Awards from Scout associations of other nations if knot is awarded
[18] Also may be worn by adults who have received a Scout or Explorer religious emblem as a youth.

Knot devices were first introduced in 1957. The original knot devices include Cub Scout, Boy Scout, Exploring (CAW[19]), Sea Explorer, and Commissioner. In 1958 the Exploring program changed and a new device was developed known as Exploring Circle V, which replaced the Exploring CAW. Then in 1958 Air Explorer the device was added. Distinguished Eagle was added in 1969. The Explorer program again changed in 1971 when the Exploring (Big E) replaced the Exploring (CAW). All remaining devices where added starting in 1985. The chapter on devices has a complete list of all devices.

---

[19] Compass, anchor, wings.

Ribbon Bars of the BSA

Honor Medal

Not current – issued 1934 ~ 1946.

Issued to represent the award of the Honor Medal for Lifesaving.

Size is 1 3/8" long by ¼" wide bearing a section of the decoration ribbon.

Silver Buffalo Award

Not current – issued 1934 ~ 1946.

Worn representing the Silver Buffalo Award.

Size is 1 3/8" long by ¼" wide bearing a section of the decoration ribbon.

Silver Antelope Award

Not current – issued 1944 ~ 1946.

Worn representing the Silver Antelope Award.

Size is 1 3/8" long by 15/32" wide bearing a section of the decoration ribbon.

Silver Beaver Award

Not current – issued 1942 ~ 1946.

Worn representing the Silver Beaver Award.

Size is 1 3/8" long by 15/32" wide bearing a section of the decoration ribbon.

Not current – issued 1934 ~ 1942.

This was the original Silver Beaver Award.

Size is 1 3/8" long by ¼" wide bearing a section of the decoration ribbon.

Eagle Scout Award

Not current – issued 1942 ~ 1946.

Worn representing the Eagle Scout award. This was the last Eagle Scout Bar that was issued prior to knots becoming the award recognition device for the Boy Scouts.

Size is 1 3/8" long by 15/32" wide bearing a section of the decoration ribbon.

Not current – issued 1934 ~ 1942.

This was the original Eagle Scout Bar.

Size is 1 3/8" long by ¼" wide bearing a section of the decoration ribbon.

Quartermaster Award

Not current – issued 1934 ~ 1946.

Worn representing the Quartermaster award from Sea Scouts.

Size is 1 3/8" long by ¼" wide bearing a section of the decoration ribbon.

Scoutmaster's Key

Not current – issued 1934 ~ 1946.

Research shows that this is the size issued from 1934 ~ 1946.

Worn representing the Scoutmaster's Key. This was the last Scoutmaster's Key Bar that was issued prior to knots becoming the award recognition device for the Boy Scouts of America.

Size is 7/8" long by ¼" wide bearing a section of the decoration ribbon.

The information on this bar comes from *The Scout Executive* stating the size of the bar, which was printed between 1934 ~ 1941. *The Scout Executive* Catalog states: "Size is 1 3/8" long by ¼" wide bearing a section of the decoration ribbon." The ribbon was not this wide, and there is conjecture that there never was a Scoutmaster's Key bar the same size as the other ribbon bars. Research indicates that the only size bar for this award is that shown and information published was a misprint and corrected when the error was discovered.

Scouter's Training Award

Not current – issued 1934 ~ 1946.

Research shows that this is the size issued from 1934 ~ 1946.

Worn representing the Scouter's Training Award. This was the last Scouter's Training Award Bar that was issued prior to knots becoming the award recognition device for the Boy Scouts of America.

Size is 7/8" long by ¼" wide bearing a section of the decoration ribbon.

The information on this bar comes from *The Scout Executive* stating the size of the bar, which was printed between 1934 ~ 1941. *The Scout Executive* Catalog states: "Size is 1 3/8" long by ¼" wide bearing a section of the decoration ribbon." The Ribbon was not this wide, and there is conjecture that there never was a Scouter's Training Award bar the same size as the other ribbon bars. Research indicates that the only size bar for this award is that shown and information published was a misprint and corrected when the error was discovered.

Knot Awards of the BSA

Honor Medal

Current – issued 2006 ~ present.

Style of knot was changed.

Recognition may be given to a member of the Boy Scouts of America, Cub Scout, Boy Scout, Varsity Scout, Venturer, Sea Scout, or any adult leader – where the evidence presented to the National Court of Honor, in accordance with prescribed regulations, shows that he or she saved or attempted to save life under circumstances that indicate heroism and risk of his or her own life. The court will give consideration to resourcefulness and to demonstrated skill in rescue methods.

In no case shall recognition be given where it appears that the risk involved was merely in the performance of duty or the meeting of an obligation because of responsibility to supervise and give leadership to the person or people whose lives were saved.

It shall be wholly within the discretion of the National Court of Honor to determine from the evidence presented which lifesaving award, if any, shall be made. Awards are issued in the name of the Boy Scouts of America.

The Honor Medal with crossed palms may be awarded to a youth member or adult leader who had demonstrated unusual heroism and skill in saving or attempting to save life with considerable risk to self.

Not current – issued 1988 ~ 2006.

Border color change to match new uniform.

Not current – issued 1983 ~ 1988.

Background color change to match a new uniform.

Not current – issued 1946 ~ 1983.

Knots issued 1946 ~ 1966 were on a coarse twill and 1966 ~ 1983 on a fine twill.

Silver World Award

Current – issued 2002 ~ present.

Issued with a smaller size circle and length of red and white stripes.

The Silver World Award was conceived in 1971. The BSA presents the award to world citizens who give outstanding service to their nation's youth or to young people in other countries. Award recipients must be citizens of countries whose Scout associations are members of the World Scout Conference. United States citizens may receive the recognition only if they are NOT registered members of the BSA.

Not current – issued 1971 ~ 2002.

This knot has been issued with both wide and narrow red stripes.

Silver Buffalo Award

Current – issued 1988 ~ present.

Color change of border and background. The intermediate knot color was not issued because there were sufficient patches on stock to last.

The Silver Buffalo Award was created in 1926. It is bestowed upon those who give truly noteworthy and extraordinary service to youth. This award, Scouting's highest commendation, recognizes the invaluable contributions that outstanding American men and women render to youth. The service must be national in character and can be directly connected with the BSA or independent of the movement.

The first Silver Buffalo Award was conferred upon Lord Baden-Powell, founder of the Scouting movement and Chief Scout of the World. The second went to the unknown scout who helped in the London fog. Mr. Boyce was so impressed that he sought out Baden Powell, learned of the Boy Scouts, and in 1910, helped bring Scouting to the United States of America.

This is the only award, other than the Silver World, that can be presented to a recipient that is not a member of the BSA. Professional Scouters are eligible for this award.

Not current – issued 1946 ~ 1988.

Silver Antelope Award

Current – issued 1988 ~ present.

Border color change to match new uniform.

The Silver Antelope Award, created in 1942 and first awarded in 1944, is granted for outstanding service to youth within the territory of a BSA region. The criteria are similar to those for the Silver Buffalo, with one major difference: A recipient must be a registered adult member of the BSA. Retired professional Scouters are eligible after 5 years.

The awards are presented in connection with regional meetings or at other public functions within the region. The National Court of Honor bestows Silver Antelope Awards on the basis of the number of registered volunteers within a region.

Not current – issued 1983 ~ 1988.

Background color change to match a new uniform.

Not current – issued 1946 ~ 1983.

Silver Beaver Award

Current – issued 2013 ~ present.

Border color change.

Established in 1931, the Silver Beaver Award is presented for distinguished service to young people within a BSA local council. The awards are bestowed at appropriate local functions. Silver Beaver awards are presented on the basis of the number of units in a council. Retired professional Scouters are eligible after 5 years.

Recipients of the Silver Fawn (awarded 1971 ~ 1974) wear the Silver Beaver knot.

Not current – issued 2002 ~ 2013.

Border color change.

Not current – issued 1988 ~ 2002.

Border color change to match new uniform.

Not current – issued 1983 ~ 1988.

Background color change to match a new uniform. This patch replaced the remaining four patches.

Not current – issued 1946 ~ 1983.

Designed for wear on the Boy Scout uniform.

Not current – issued 1966 ~ 1979.

Designed for wear on the Explorer uniform.

Not current – issued 1966 ~ 1979.

Designed for wear on the Sea Explorer white uniform.

Not current – issued 1951 ~ 1979.

Border color change from black to blue.

Designed for wear on the Sea Explorer blue and Cub Scout uniforms. Information comes from an unknown Scouter who stated that the only knots available in 1950 were those made on khaki.

Also worn by recipients of the Silver Fawn, issued 1971 ~ 1974.

Misprint – issued in reverse order.

Note the blue loop over white. White ends are always on the left (as worn – right as viewed) and the loop going over is always on the right (as worn – left as viewed). This knot is reversed.

This knot was only made with a cloth back. This is most likely the second issue of the knot and a change from black to blue border would have occurred with this issue.

Not current – issued 1951.

This knot was only made with a cloth back and a black border. This is most likely the original issue of this knot.

District Award of Merit

Current – 1980 ~ present.

Background color change from royal blue to blue.

This is the only non-square knot – knot; correct position is the open ends down, as pictured.

A council level award presented upon recommendation of the district. It is based on a maximum of one award per year for each 25 units or portion thereof. For example if there are 26-50 units, then the district may recommend 2 awards for that year.

The District Award of Merit is awarded by a District to volunteer and professional adults for service to youth in the District. Normally, the award is presented for service to youth in excess of five years.

A person may receive more than one District/Division Award of Merit, although there are no provisions for the wearing of a device or emblem officially to denote the second or subsequent awards.

The BSA has no records of any volunteer or professional earning the District Award of Merit in more than three separate Districts.

Career members of the Boy Scouts of America may receive this award upon concurrence of the Council Scout Executive and the Director of Operations at the National office, BSA.

Candidates for this award must be nominated. Self-nomination disqualifies the candidate.

Requirements:

A nominee must be a registered Scouter.

A nominee must have rendered noteworthy service to youth in Scouting, outside of Scouting, or both.

Note: The nature and value of "noteworthy service to youth" may consist of a single plan or decisions that contributed vitally to the lives of large numbers of youth or it may have been given to a small group over an extended period of time.

Consideration must be given to the nominee's Scouting position and the corresponding opportunity to render outstanding service beyond the expectations of that Scouting position.

The nominee's attitude toward and cooperation with the district, division, and/or council is to be taken into consideration.

Not current – issued 1975 ~ 1980.

Background color change from navy blue to royal blue.

Not current – issued 1973 ~ 1975.

Order of the Arrow Distinguished Service Award

Current – issued 2007 ~ present.

Style of the knot was changed.

The Order of the Arrow Distinguished Service Award is presented to individuals for outstanding cheerful service to the Order of the Arrow and Scouting over a significant period of time at any level beyond the local Lodge level.

The Award is presented at the National Order of the Arrow Conference every two years.

Not current – issued 1977 ~ 2007.

Heroism Award

Not current – issued 1992 ~ 2012.

Color change of knot from red to light red. The shape of the knot was also changed.

Award was discontinued in December 2012.

Recognition had been given to a youth member or adult leader, where the evidence presented to the National Court of Honor, in accordance with prescribed regulations, who had demonstrated heroism and skill in saving or attempting to save life with minimal risk to self.

Not current – issued 1982 ~ 1992.

Medal of Merit

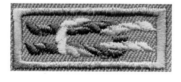

Current – issued 2002 ~ present.

Border, background, knot color, and style of knot change.

Recognition may be given to a youth member or adult leader where the evidence presented to the National Court of Honor, in accordance with prescribed regulations, shows that a significant or outstanding act of service or exceptional character was performed. That action taken need not involve attempts of rescue or risk to self but must put into practice Scouting skills and/or ideals. Recognition shall not be given where it appears that the action involved was merely in the performance of duty or the meeting of an obligation.

The Medal of Merit may be awarded to a youth member or adult leader who has performed some outstanding act of service or of rare or exceptional character that reflects an uncommon degree of concern for the well being of others.

Not current – issued 2002.

Border, background, and knot color change. Also issued with logo on plastic back.

Not current – issued 1988 ~ 2002.

Border color change to match new uniform.

Not current – issued 1983 ~ 1988.

Background color change to match a new uniform and change in color of knot.

Not current – issued prior to 1953 ~ 1983.

NOTE: This knot was approved in 1952, however there is no evidence that it was manufactured and sold prior to 1953.

Arrow of Light Award

Current – issued 1983 ~ present.

The Arrow of Light is worn by Scouters that completed the Arrow of Light requirements as a Cub Scout.

Not current – issued 1979 ~ 1983.

Not Current – patch issued by mistake – 1989 ~ 1990.

Note: The over loop is green (mistake) instead of red (correct).

The vendor inadvertently reversed the colors of the knot on this patch. This knot (error) was shown in Scouting Magazine in October 1989 with the overloop on the right side (as viewed), and the colors for the knot in the correct position.

Eagle Scout Award

Current – issued 2013 ~ present.

Border color change.

Recipients of the Eagle Scout Award wear this patch. Palms can be worn on the patch to indicate the number of additional palm awards that the Eagle Scout has earned.

There are 3 additional devices that can be worn on the Eagle Scout Award. A gold eagle pin can also be worn on this patch to indicate the recipient received the Distinguished Eagle (see device on page 55). A second device was created for recipients of the National Outstanding Eagle Scout Award [(NOESA) see device on page 58]. A third recognition was created for the Outstanding Eagle Scout project of the year (see device on page 57 - 58). This recognition "The Adams Award" is in three different colors. A bronze device for council award, a gold device for region award and a silver device for a national award.

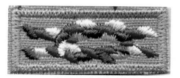

Not current – issued 1988 ~ 2002 & 2003 ~ 2013.

Border color change.

Not current – issued 2002 ~ 2003.

Border color change to match new uniform.

Not current – issued 1983 ~ 1988.

Background color change to match a new uniform. This patch replaced the remaining four patches.

Not current – issued 1947 ~ 1983.

Designed for wear on the Boy Scout uniform.

Not current – issued 1966 ~ 1979.

Designed for wear on the Explorer uniform.

Not current – issued 1966 ~ 1979.

Designed for wear on the Sea Explorer white uniform.

Not current – issued 1966 ~ 1979.

Designed for wear on the Sea Explorer blue and Cub Scout uniforms.

Eagle Scout NESA Life Membership Award

Current – issued 2008 ~ present.

This award is a recognition that an adult Scouter continues to support Eagle Scouts at the highest level though a National Eagle Scout Association (NESA) life membership.

Once an Eagle Scout life membership is processed by NESA, an adult scouter will be eligible to wear this knot.

NOTE: Only 1 knot may be worn representing Eagle Scout. If this knot is worn, the Eagle Scout knot must be removed.

Not current – issued 2008.

This knot was issued and recalled by National Supply because the knot was 2" long instead of 1⅞" long.

Quartermaster Award

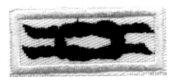

Current – issued 2007 ~ present.

Style of knot was changed.

This patch is worn by recipients of the Quartermaster Award.

The Quartermaster Award is the highest award that may be earned in the Sea Scout program. Youth can earn the award prior to their 21st birthday. Both boys and girls in the Sea Scout program may earn this award.

Not current – issued 1954 ~ 2007.

This patch was originally issued to wear on the Sea Explorer white uniform, however in 1979 became the only knot issued for the Quartermaster Award.

Not current – issued 1947 ~ 1979.

Patch was issued for wear on the Boy Scout uniform.

Not current – issued 1954 ~ 1979.

Patch was issued for wear on the blue Sea Explorer uniform. This patch replaced the one shown below.

Not current – issued 1951 ~ 1954.

Patch was issued for wear on the blue Sea Explorer uniform. Due to the color combination (the knot being of poor contrast with the background and nearly invisible), this patch deleted from inventory. It was replaced with the one shown above.

Ranger Award

Not current – issued 1950 ~ 1951.

Patch was issued for wear on the Explorer uniform.

This was the top award in the Explorer Scout (Ranger) program.

The Ranger award was the top award in the original Exploring program.

There have been reports of various color background colors ranging from tan to light yellow. All knots discovered with these background colors have been used. This could be from washing over the years. The only officially manufactured knot is the one shown.

Air Scout Ace Award / Air Explorer Ace Award

Not current – issued 1950 ~ 1954.

This was issued for recipients of the Air Explorer Ace (and previous Air Scout Ace) Award. This was the top award in the Air Scout/Explorer program.

Silver Award (1st)

Not current – issued 1950 ~ 1954.

This knot was issued for the first Silver Award. It was the top award in the Exploring program.

Silver Award (2nd) / Explorer Silver Award / Explorer Achievement Award / Young American Award / Exploring Gold Award / G.O.L.D. (Growth Opportunity in Leadership Development) Award

Not current – issued 2002 ~ 2012.

Border change on this knot issue. There is also a lighter color silver used for the knot and border. This is the current knot issued through the supply system.

It should be noted that although this knot is not listed in the catalogs or council order books, it is still available in the supply system.

The shape of this knot (ends pointed inward) has been used on this knot from the original knot issued in 1954 until now. There was a variation shown below that was issued in the 1990's that was different.

The knot award was issued for the second Silver Award from 1954 ~ 1966. That knot had a cloth backing.

The Silver Award was discontinued from the basic Explorer program in 1958, after which all Explorers were then able to earn the Eagle Scout Award. Air Explorers continued to earn the Silver Award until 1966. Although the knot was discontinued from the catalogs in 1966, it remained available through the supply system.

The knot was re-listed in the insignia catalog and renamed as the Explorer Silver Award from 1976 ~ 1986.

It was still designated for wear to represent those who have earned the Ranger, Air Explorer Ace, or the Explorer Silver Awards.

The knot was again renamed from 1986 ~ 1994 as the Explorer Achievement Award. During this period of time, it was also designated for wear to represent those who have earned the Ranger, Air Explorer Ace, and Explorer Silver Award.

The next designation for this award was the Young American Award – 1995 ~ 1996. Also representing all previous awards.

The knot was again renamed, from 1996 ~ 1999, as the Exploring Gold Award or the G.O.L.D. (Growth Opportunity in Leadership Development) Award. It was also designated for wear to represent those who have earned the Ranger, Air Explorer Ace, Explorer Silver, Young American Award, and the Explorer Achievement award.

There is no device to distinguish which award was earned.

Only those who earned the award through the Exploring Division of the Boy Scouts prior to August 1998 may wear this award.

Note: Exploring became a subsidiary as of August 1998 and awards of the Boy Scouts are not authorized to be awarded through the new Exploring program.

Not current – issued 1954 ~ 1966 & 1976 ~ 1998.

This is the original shape of knot and border issued.

It should be noted that the dates listed above are for the listings in the insignia guide catalogs. The knot award was available from the supply system from 1954 to present.

There have been some variations in the color of the knot from gray to pink to rose gray.

Not current.

This is a variation on the knot. Note the ends of the knot with a difference in the way they point. This is the standard shape knot for most awards.

This variation occurred in the 1990's.

Venturing Silver Award

Current – issued 2002 ~ present.

Change in color and shape of knot.

Recipients of the Venturing Silver Award wear this knot on their uniform.

This is the highest award in the Venturing program.

Not current – issued 1998 ~ 2002.

William T. Hornaday Award for Distinguished Service in Conservation

Current – issued 1991 ~ present.

The Hornaday Award was established in 1914 as a conservation awards program to inspire members of the BSA to work constructively for conservation. **The knot is only authorized for Scouts who have earned the bronze or silver medal and for Scouters who have earned the gold medal.** All issues of the Hornaday Awards are listed to provide information on the award.[20]

There are a number of awards that may be presented.

The **unit certificate** is submitted to your local council service center, on a completed application for the unit award. The local council will then forward the application to the national office of the Boy Scouts of America. The project description form should indicate the category of the project—soil and water conservation, fish and wildlife management, forestry and range management, energy conservation, air and water pollution control, resource recovery, or hazardous material disposal and management; the specific title of the project; and a detailed description of what was done, who did it, when it was done, and how it was done. Be sure to include any other pertinent information.

The **bronze badge** is awarded to individuals. A Scout or Venturer completes the application for the badge and submits it to their local council service center. The local council will then forward the application to the national office of the Boy Scouts of America. Be certain the applicant and the conservation adviser sign the application before it is sent to the council office. Be sure to check and date all merit badges completed. The project description form should give a detailed description of the project as indicated under the unit award above. Boy Scout and Varsity Scout applicants must complete these requirements before their 18th birthday. Venturer applicants must complete requirements before their 21st birthday. Following council approval, the application is forwarded to director of Ourdoor Programs, Boy Scouts of America.

The **bronze medal** is awarded by the National Council upon recommendation of the local council. A qualified Boy Scout, Varsity Scout, or Venturer must apply through and be recommended by his or her local council. Final selection is made by a national William T. Hornaday Award selection committee, and presentation is made by the local council.

The **silver medal** is handled in the same way as the bronze medal in regard to recommendation and application. The award is the highest possible attainment in conservation for a Boy Scout, Varsity Scout, or Venturer.

The **gold medal** may be considered when a qualified Scouter is recommended by his or her council, by an established conservation organization, or by any recognized conservationist. The nominee must have demonstrated leadership and a commitment of education of youth on a national or international level, reflecting the natural resource conservation/environmental awareness mission of the Boy Scouts of

---

[20] Information from Boy Scouts of America's web site www.scouting.org

America.

Nominations must be approved by the BSA's national conservation committee. The gold medal is the highest possible attainment in conservation for a Scouter.

The **gold badge** is awarded by the local council's conservation committee. Scouters who have demonstrated leadership and a significant commitment to conservation and the education of Scouting youth on a council or district level over a sustained period (at least three years) may be nominated for this award. Councils may obtain gold badges by sending approved award applications to the Boy Scout Conservation Service at the national office.

NOTE: The knot award is only worn by recipients of the bronze medal, silver medal, or gold medal.

Speaker Bank Award

Not current – Issued 2008 ~ 2011.

This is for recognition of completion of 20 presentations of an approved program. The presentations must be for fundraising or promotion of the Scouting program. Scout/Scouter training is not considered part of this award.

Not current – issued 2008.

This knot was issued and recalled by National Supply because the knot was 2" long instead of 1⅞" long.

Distinguished Commissioner Service Award

Current – issued 1987 ~ present.

The Distinguished Commissioner Service Award was instituted to upgrade the commissioner service and to recognize commissioners who are providing quality service.

Award is presented to commissioners, upon recommendation, for completing the following requirements:

- Complete training as outlined by the local council, including earning the Commissioner's Key.

- Serve as an active commissioner for five consecutive years and be currently registered with the Boy Scouts of America.

- Recharter at least 90% of the units in your area of service for a minimum of the past two consecutive years. This applies to council commissioners, assistant council commissioners, district commissioners, assistant district commissioners, and unit commissioners.

- Assist units so that more than 50% achieve National Quality Unit Award in your area of service for a minimum of the past two consecutive years.

   Note: Although the National Quality Unit Award has been replaced by the Journey to Excellence, requirements for this award has not been updated as of the date of this printing.

- Roundtable commissioner recognition is based on completing the first two requirements, and must conduct at least nine roundtables per year for the past two years.

Local councils certify the eligibility of individuals, and present the recognition. There is no national application.

Doctorate of Commissioner Science Knot Award

Current – issued 2008 ~ present.

This knot is currently being issued in 2 different styles. The type 3 knot as shown and the type 1 knot as shown below. Both types being issued are the correct size for the knot award.

Tenure

Serve as a commissioner for a minimum of 5 years. Their service can be in one or more commissioner roles or positions of service.

Training

A. Bachelors of Commissioner Science Degree (BCS)

Prerequisites

1. Maintain registration in any capacity as a Commissioner during the entire training program listed below.
2. Complete commissioner basic training.

Course requirements

Complete a minimum of seven (7) courses of instruction, and at least five (5) of the courses at the Bachelor's program level as listed in the *Continuing Education for Commissioners* manual.

Performance

1. Approval of Council Commissioner or assigned Assistant Council Commissioner.
2. Approval of Scout Executive or Advisor to Commissioner Service.

B. Master of Commissioner Science Degree (MCS)

Prerequisites

1. Completion of bachelor's degree.
2. Earned Arrowhead Honor.
3. Current registration as a commissioner.

Course requirements

Complete a minimum of seven (7) additional courses of instruction (total of 14), and at least seven (7) of the courses at the Master's program level as listed in the *Continuing Education for*

Commissioners manual.

Performance

1. Approval of Council Commissioner or assigned Assistant Council Commissioner.

2. Approval of Scout Executive or Advisor to Commissioner Service.

C. Doctor of Commissioner Science Degree (DCS)

Prerequisites

1. Completion of master's degree.

2. Have been awarded the Commissioner's Key.

3. Current registration as a commissioner.

Course requirements

Complete a minimum of ten (10) additional courses of instruction (total of 24), and at least five (5) of the courses at the Doctor's program level as listed in the *Continuing Education for Commissioners* manual.

Thesis or Project

1. Completion of a thesis or project on any topic of value ot Scouting in the local council.

2. The topic and final paper or project must be approved by the council commissioner, or assigned assistant council commissioner, or the dean of the doctorate program and the staff advisor for commissioner service.

Performance

1. Serve on the College of Commissioner Science Faculty (instructor or support staff) or work with training support for commissioners for at least one year.

2. Recruit at least three new commissioners at any level.

3. Approval of Council Commissioner or assigned Assistant Council Commissioner.

4. Approval of Scout Executive or Advisor to Commissioner Science.

Grandfather or Sunset Clause

Since the key requirement of this award is tied to an approval of a Thesis (Councils with a Commissioner's College) or Project (Councils without a Commissioners College) that is only earned once, this award is retroactive for individuals who have completed other requirements prior to the approval of this award. This clause applies for the previous 10 years. Any commissioner who meets these requirements would need to list any courses they have completed previously and then complete their thesis or project to apply for the award.

Not current – issued 2008.

This knot was issued and recalled by National Supply because the knot was 2" long instead of 1⅞" long.

Commissioner Award of Excellence in Unit Service

Current – issued 2013 ~ present.

Change in type of knot.

Requirements

Any registered Commissioner who is providing direct unit service is eligible to earn the **Commissioner Award of Excellence in Unit Service**, through unit service and a project that results in improved retention of members and on-time unit recharter, over the course of two consecutive years. If a Commissioner who is not registered as a Unit Commissioner wishes to earn this award, they must work with the District Commissioner where the unit(s) is/are registered.

The Commissioner shall consistently demonstrate the following:

1. The ability to use UVTS 2.0 to log unit visits.

2. The ability to provide UVTS 2.0 visit reports to an ADC or DC.

Performance

Complete each item below:

A. **Performance Goal**: Through utilization of the Annual Unit Self-Assessment tool, identify a specific goal in a specific unit that would result in higher quality unit performance. The goal should target improvement in at least one of the Unit Self-Assessment target areas.

B. **Action Plan**: Provide a written plan to achieve the goal indentified in Section A.

   Have the plan approved by the Unit Leader, with Unit Leader's signature.

C. **Results**

   1. Unit Self-Assessment conducted twice a year for two years.

   2. Unit Retention: On-time rechartering for two consecutive years.

   3. Youth Retention: Youth retention percentages must show improvement.

Participation

1. Be a participant or staff member in ONE continuing education event for Commissioner Service[21]. For example: District, Council, Area, Regional or National College of Commissioner Science, Commissioner Conference, Philmont, Sea Base, or Summit training.

---

[21] Participation or staffing in a continuing education event as noted above, prior to the start date of this award, shall not be applied. Participation or instructing during training sessions as part of regular staff meetings may not be applied.

2. The Commissioner shall make at least (6) physical visits to each assigned unite per year. All visits must be logged with UVTS 2.0. Examples: unit meetings, unit activities, leader meetings, and summer camp visitations.

3. The Commissioner shall make at least (6) significant contacts (in addition to those made in item 2,) for each unit serviced, by telephone, two-way electronic communication, or in person. These contacts must be logged in UVTS 2.0.

Training and Experience

Compete each item below:

1. Commissioner Basic Training date:

2. Provide rechartering service, by holding membership inventories, training verification, and "*Journey to Excellence*"[22] progress review meetings. Perform charter presentations to the Chartered Organizations of the units you serve.

NOTE: A commissioner may earn this award up to three times, while registered as a commissioner at any level. Devices are added for the second and third award.

Not current – issued 2012.

This knot is slightly oversize.

George Meany Award

Not current – issued 1987 ~ 2011.

The George Meany Award recognizes union members – men and women – who have made a significant contribution to the youth of their communities by volunteering in the programs of the BSA[23]. This was the first award authorized for a community organization, therefore the knot was issued for specifically for the AFL-CIO union organization.

Not current – issued 1987, Patch issued by mistake.

Note the over loop is on the white background field. White is never the main color when 2 colors are present. Over loop should be on the red side.

Community Organization Award

Current – issued 2001 ~ present.

In recent years, representatives of several national chartered organizations have inquired about the development of a recognition which could be given to registered adult leaders in units chartered in community organizations; similar to the adult religious awards presented by the various denominations and faith groups. After study and evaluation, the BSA National Court of Honor approved the concept of a Community Organization Award square

---

[22] Unit-Specific requirements and performance criteria are founded on BSA's Journey to Excellence guidelines. As changes are incorporated, the Council Commissioner must scope impacts and adjust expectations as required.
[23] Information obtained from Boy Scouts of America publication # 86-011.

knot. This square knot would be available to be worn by uniformed Scouters who have been recognized for their service to Scouting youth in the community.

As of February 24, 2014 there ware eighteen awards that fall into this classification:

- Marvin M. Lewis Award of the Benevolent and Protective Order of the Elks (BPOE);

- Daniel Carter Beard Masonic Scouter Award;

- Veterans of Foreign Wars Scouter's Achievement Award;

- American Legion Scouting Square Knot Award;

- Department of Defense – United States Military Outstanding Volunteer Service Medal;

- Herbert G. Horton Alpha Phi Omega (AΦΩ) Youth Service Award of the Alpha Phi Omega national service fraternity;

- Cliff Dochterman Award of the International Rotarians Fellowship of Scouting;

- Ruritan National Scout Leader Service Award of the Ruritan National Service Club;

- Raymond A. Finley Sea Scout Service Award of the U.S. Power Squadron;

- AMVETS BSA Youth Outreach Award;

- Lions Clubs International Scouting Service Award;

- National Society of the Sons of the American Revolution Robert E. Burt Boy Scout Volunteer Award;

- Alpha Phi Alpha (AΦA) Fraternity Good Turn Service Award;

- Military Order of the World Wars;

- Nonprofit Leadership Alliance H. Roe Bartle Training Award;

- Philmont Staff Association Silver Sage Award;

- Woods Services Award for Scouting with Special Needs; and

- George Meany Award of the American Federation of the Labor & Congress of Industrial Organizations (AFL-CIO). This award is part of this category, but retained the use of the original square knot designed for the Meany award until the end of 2011, after which it was incorporated into the Community Organization Award.

Community Organization Award is a generic term used by the BSA to identify a category of awards used by secular, national, or community organizations to recognize their members for voluntary service and achievement. The organization must also be a BSA national chartered organization.

This knot resembles the William H. Spurgeon III Award knot. The background color is purple, while the Spurgeon knot was issued in 3 background colors over the years: olive, green, and black.

William H. Spurgeon III Award

Not current – issued 2006 ~ 2012.

Background color change – background changed from black to light olive green. Also the knot style changed.

This award was presented to adult Exploring leaders, businesses, and organizations at both the local and national level for service in support of the Exploring program. Only holders of individual awards may wear the knot (not officers or employees of a firm that received the award).

Candidates for this award must be nominated.

Self-nomination disqualifies the candidate.

Only those who were awarded through the Exploring Division of the Boy Scouts of America prior to August 1,1998 may wear this award.

Note: Exploring became a subsidiary as of August 1, 1998 and knot awards of the Boy Scouts are not authorized to be awarded through the new Exploring program.

Not current – issued 2002 ~ 2006.

Background color change – background changed from olive green to black.

Not current – issued 1988 ~ 2002.

Initial traditional size knot issued. This knot has an olive-green background.

Not current – issued 1988.

This oversized knot was the initial knot issued. Because it did not match the size of all other knots, it was immediately replaced.

Whitney M. Young Jr. Award

Current – issued 2004 ~ present.

Style of knot changed from type 1 to type 3

Several years ago BSA was concerned that certain rural and inner-city urban areas were not being reached by the Scouting program. As part of its push to offer the Scouting program to rural and inner-city areas, the Whitney Young, Jr. Award was developed to recognize outstanding support and service at both the local and national level in reaching under-served areas.

The knot may only be worn by holders of individual awards.

Candidates for this award must be nominated. Self-nomination disqualifies the candidate.

 Not current – issued 1988 ~ 2004.

Asian American Spirit of Scouting Service Award

 Current – issued 2013 ~ present.

This knot is a misprint. The colors were reversed – note the over loop should be white.

This award is used to recognize outstanding service by an adult for demonstrated involvement in the development and implementation of Scouting opportunities for Asian American youth. The award can also be presented to an organization, but the knot cannot be worn unless it is an individual award.

National Scoutreach committee approves the award upon nomination by council. The council's annual quota of awards shall not exceed the number of districts in the council.

 Not current – issued 2013.

Color change on the background and style of knot.

 Not current – issued 2009 ~ 2013.

 Not current – issued 2004 ~ 2009

This knot is a misprint. The colors were reversed – note the over loop – it should be white. Most of the misprints were destroyed and a new order placed. The re-order came in the same as the original and was issued.

¡Scouting…Vale La Pena! Service Award

 Current – issued 2014 ~ present.

This award is used to recognize outstanding service by an adult for demonstrated involvement in the development and implementation of Scouting opportunities for Hispanic American/Latino youth. The award can also be presented to an organization, but the knot cannot be worn unless it is an individual award.

National Scoutreach committee approves the award upon nomination by council. The council's annual quota of awards shall not exceed the number of districts in the council.

Note: This is the first knot issued with the correct order of colors. Notice the yellow over loop.

Not current - issued 2009 ~ 2013.

This knot is a misprint. The colors are reversed. The over loop should be yellow.

Not current – issued 2004 ~ 2009.

This knot is a misprint. The colors were reversed and the silver-blue is the wrong color. Note the over loop – it should be yellow. This knot was issued.

Not current – issued 2004.

This knot is a misprint. The colors were reversed – note the over loop – it should be yellow. Most of this misprint was destroyed. Only a few were issued.

Venturing Leadership Award

Current – issued 2004 ~ present.

The Venturing Leadership Award is presented by councils, areas/regions, and the BSA National Council to Venturers who have made exceptional contributions to Venturing and who exemplify the Venturing Code and Oath.

Councils may present two awards for youth per year for up to 50 crews/ships and one additional youth award per year for each fraction of 25 crews/ships above 50. Regions may present 12 youth awards per year. National may present six youth awards per year.

Although adults were able to receive this award when it first started, effective 2011, only youth may receive this award.

Philmont Training Center Masters Track Award

Current – Issued 2008 ~ present.

The Philmont Training Center Masters Track Award is presented to Scouters who attend the Philmont Training Center (PTC) at any level of training.

Purpose

> To offer continuing educational opportunities, so that Scouters have incentives to return, over a number of years, to take advanced training at the Training Center, and to be able to take their knowledge back to units, districts, councils, council clusters, national, and international venues to benefit Scouts and Scouters.

Note: All actions for the Philmont Training Center Masters Track Square Knot must be earned after June 1, 2008. All courses taken prior to this date will not be counted.

To earn the PTC Masters Track Award, the Scouter must:

First Track:

- Attend the Philmont Training Center as a participant.

    Note: Participants would earn a Philmont Training Center Conference

Patch.

Second Track:

- Take an additional course at Philmont Training Center.

  And

- Recruit 3 people to attend a Philmont Training Center course.

  And

- Teach a BSA course in your:

  District, Council, Area, or Region (Course and participation in the course must be approved by the Council or Area raining Chairperson prior to working on the course.

  Note: Participants would earn a Philmont Training Center Square Knot.

- Upon the completion of Track 2, the participant should contact the PTC by letter to request the needed verification to purchase the square knot and for your certificate.

Third Track:

- Do one of the following two items:

  1. Serve as a Faculty Member on the Philmont Training Center Course.

     Or

  2. Attend an additional training course at the PTC.

     And

  3. Recruit at least 3 people who attend a Training Center course.

- Do the first requirement and one of the following 3 items:

  1. Coordinate a Council, Area, or regional Cluster approved Training Event.

     And

  2. Coordinate and Staff a promotional booth for the PTC at a Council Event,

     Or

  3. Conduct a Council, "Philmont Family Meeting" to share PTC information and encourage family participation,

     Or

  4. Teach a training course in a foreign country – Coordinated and approved by the BSA International Division.

  Note: Participants would earn a Philmont Training Center Square Knot Device.

Not current – issued 2008.

This knot was issued and recalled by National Supply because the knot was 2" long instead of 1⅞" long.

William D. Boyce New-Unit Organizer Award

Current – issued 2009 ~ present.

Change in knot style.

The William D. Boyce New-Unit Organizer Award is to recognize volunteers who organize one or more traditional Scouting units.

The award is a square knot representing the three phases of our program – Cub Scouting, Boy Scouting, and Venturing.

The knot is earned by organizing one traditional unit. A program device is earned for each additional unit organized, allowing the award to recognize a volunteer for organizing up to four new units.

The award program is administered by the Relationships Division and awards are presented by local councils.

Requirements

1) With the approval of the district committee chair, serve as the organizer and complete the successful organization of one new traditional unit (Cub Scout pack, Boy Scout troop, Varsity Scout team, or Venturing crew).

2) Organize the unit by following all procedures as published in the "New-Unit Organization Process," No. 34196, particularly ensuring that new unit leadership is trained, program for the new unit is organized and has begun, the new unit committee if functioning, a unit commissioner is assigned, all paperwork for the new unit is completed and processed, and the unit charter is presented to the chartered organization.

3) Sometimes several individuals help to organize a new unit. However, for this award only one volunteer can be recognized as the organizer of each new unit.

4) A program device can be earned and worn on the new-unit organizer knot for each additional unit organized. The program device would represent the type of unit organized (a Cub Scout pack, Boy Scout troop, Varsity Scout team, or Venturing crew). The knot and up to three program devices may be worn, representing recognition for organizing the total of four new traditional units. Multiple program devices form the same program may be earned and worn.

5) The new-unit organization award recognized volunteers for organizing traditional units after, and not before, March 1, 2005.

Not current – issued 2005 ~ 2009.

This is the only knot ever issued with this shape. This shape was never approved by the national committee.

Religious Emblem (Youth) Square Knot

Current – issued 1975 ~ present.

Changed to a fully embroidered background.

There are a number of religious medals that may be earned by the youth member through their religious denomination. The square knot is worn to represent having received the award through their religious affillation.

Miniature device(s) is/are worn with the youth religious emblem square knot indicating the emblem(s) earned as a youth. See chapter on devices starting on page 53 of this book.

Not current – issued 1971 ~ 1975.

There was a twill/weave background initially used for this knot award.

Religious Emblem (Adult) Square Knot

Current – issued 1973 ~ present.

Scouters may be presented an award from their church. This knot is worn to represent receipt of a religious award presented by their religious affillation.

Scoutmaster's Key / Scouter's Key

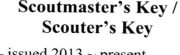

Current – issued 2013 ~ present.

Border color change.

Name was changed from Scoutmaster's Key to Scouter's Key in 1948.

The award is currently presented to individuals in key positions (Cubmaster, Scoutmaster, Varsity Scout Coach, Venturing Advisor, Skipper, Commissioner, and District Committee). In the Explorer Advisors and Air Explorer Squadron Leaders earned the Key.

Between 1988 and 2012 the Cubmaster earned the Cubmaster award instead of the Scouter's Key.

The appropriate device(s) is/are worn on the knot to depict how the award was earned. Note – multiple devices may be worn to depict the various programs the award was issued for.

See requirements following the patches.

Not current – issued 1998 ~ 2002 & 2004 ~ 2013.

Border color change.

Not current – issued 2002 ~ 2004.

Border color change to match new uniform.

Not current – issued 1983 ~ 1988.

Background color change to match a new uniform. This patch replaced the following four patches.

Not current – issued 1946 ~ 1983.

Designed for wear on the Boy Scout uniform.

Not current – issued 1966 ~ 1979.

Designed for wear on the Explorer uniform.

Not current – issued 1966 ~ 1979.

Designed for wear on the Sea Explorer white uniform.

Not current – issued 1966 ~ 1979.

Designed for wear on the Sea Explorer blue and Cub Scout uniforms.

Requirements for the Scouter's Key are as follows:

Cubmaster's Key Requiements[24]

Tenure

Within a five-year period, complete at least three years of registered tenure as a Cubmaster or one year as a registered assistant Cubmaster plus two years as a registered Cubmaster. (This can include the tenure used to earn the Scouter's Training Award.)

Training

Do the following:

- Complete basic training for Cubmasters.
- Complete *This is Scouting* training.
- Attend a Pow Wow or University of Scouting (or equivalent), or attend at least four roundtables (or equivalent) during each year of the tenure used for this award.

Performance

Do the following during the tenure used for this award:

- Achieve at least the Silver level of Journey to Excellence for at least two years. The Quality Unit Award is acceptable if the tenure used is prior to 2011.

---

[24] Publication 511-053, 2012 Printing

- Earn the National Summertime Pack Award at least once.

- Conduct an annual pack planning session and have published pack meeting/activity schedule for the pack's parents in each year.

- Participate in at least one additional supplemental or advanced training event at the council, area, region, or national level.

Scoutmaster's Key Requirements[25]

Tenure

Complete three years of registered tenure as a Scoutmaster within a five-year period (This can include the tenure used to earn the Scouter's Award).

Training

Do the following:

- Complete basic training for Scoutmasters.

- Complete *This Is Scouting* training.

- Attend a university of Scouting (or equivalent), or attend at least four roundtables (or equivalent) during each year of the tenure used for this award.

Performance

Do the following during the tenure used for this award:

- Achieve at least the Silver level of Journey to Excellence for at least two years. The Quality Unit Award is acceptable if the tenure used is prior to 2011.

- Earn the National Outdoor Challenge Award at least one.

- Conduct an annual troop planning session and have a published troop meeting/activity schedule for the troop's parents in each year.

- Participate in at least one additional supplemental or advanced training event at the council, area, region, or national level.

Coach's Key Requirements[26]

Tenure

Complete at least three years of registered tenure as a Varsity team Coach within a five-year period. (This can include the tenure used to earn the Scouter's Training Award.)

Training

Do the following:

- Complete basic training for Coaches.

- Complete *This Is Scouting* training.

[25] Publication 511-054, Printing
[26] Publication 511-055, Printing 2012
[27] Reference web site: http://www.scouting.org/filestore/training/pdf/Sea_Scout_Skippers_Key.pdf, 2014 Printing
[28] Publication 511-056, 2012 Printing
[29] *www.scouting.org/training/adult.aspx*, District Committee Key

- Attend a university of Scouting (or equivalent), or attend at least four roundtables (or equivalent) during each year of the tenure used for this award.

Performance

Do the following during the tenure used for this award:

- Achieve at least the Silver level of Journey to Excellence for at least two years. The Quality Unit Award is acceptable if the tenure used is prior to 2011.

- Conduct an annual team planning session and have a published troop meeting/activity schedule for the team's parents in each year.

- Participate in at least one additional supplemental or advanced training event at the council, area, region, or national level.

Skipper's Key Requirements[27]

Training

Complete *Venturing Leader Youth Protection.*

Complete *Sea Scouting Adult Leader Basic Training.*

Complete a boating safety course offered by the U.S. Coast Guard Auxiliary, U.S. Power Squadron, or NASBLA approved boater safety course.

Tenure

Complete three years of registered tenure as the Skipper within a five-year period. (Time can include tenure used to earn the Scouter's Training Award.)

Performance

1. Achieve at least the Silver level of Journey to Excellence at least two years.

2. Conduct annual quarterdeck training and have a published meeting/activity schedule for the ship in each year.

3. Participate in at least one additional supplemental or advanced training event at the council, are, region, or national level.

Certification

The Ship Committee Chair and Commissioner must approve the Skipper's application for Skipper's Key.

Completed form must be sent along with $10.00 to:

Sea Scouts, BSA
ATTN: Keith Christopher
PO BOX 152079
Irving, TX 75015-2079

Account Number 79003-3030

Note: Although the Skipper's Key uses the Scouter's Key knot and Sea

Scout device, there is a different medal for this award.

Advisor's Key Requirements[28]

Tenure

Complete at least years of registered tenure as a Venturing crew Advisor within a five-year period. (This can include the tenure used to earn the Venturing Training Award.)

Training

Do the following:

- Complete basic training for Advisors.

- Complete *This Is Scouting* training.

- Attend a university of Scouting (or equivalent), or attend at least four roundtables (or equivalent) during each year of the tenure used for this award.

Performance

Do the following during the tenure used for this award:

- Achieve at least the Silver level of Journey to Excellence for at least two years. The Quality Unit Award is acceptable if the tenure used is prior to 2011.

- Have an annual crew planning session and have a published crew meeting/activity schedule for the crew in each year.

- Participate in at least one additional supplemental or advanced training event at the council, area, region, or national level.

District Committee Key Requirements[29]

Tenure

Complete at least years of registered tenure as a member of a district committee as the chair of one of the operating committees. (This can include the tenure used to earn the District Committee Training Award.)

Do the following during the tenure used for this award:

- Attend a District Committee Training Workshop.

- Complete *Staffing the District Committee* training.

- Complete *This Is Scouting* training.

Performance

Do the following during the tenure used for this award:

- Serve in a district that achieves at least the Bronze level of Journey to Excellence for at least two of the years. (The Quality District Award is acceptable if the tenure used is prior to 2011.)

- Take part actively in at least twelve district committee meetings.

- Give primary leadership in meeting at least the Silver level of at least one District Journey to Excellence objective in each year.

- Participate in at least one additional supplemental or advanced training event at the council, area, region, or national level.

Commissioner's Key Requirements

Training

Complete the Commissioner Basic Training sessions as outlined in the *Commissioner Basic Training Manual*.

Complete personal coaching orientation including the orientation projects.

Tenure

Complete three years as a registered commissioner within a five-year period.

Performance

Earn the Arrowhead Honor Award for your position.

Arrowhead Award Requirements for Council Commissioner and Assistant Council Commissioner (Field Service):

1) Work with your Scout executive or other staff adviser and evaluate all district commissioners in the council;

2) Have an active, effective district commissioner in every district of the council;

3) Develop and put into action a suitable recruiting plan throughout the council;

4) Achieve a ratio in the council of one unit commission for every three units, or a ratio approved by your staff advisor;

5) Chair or actively take part in six council commissioner meetings;

6) Give leadership to a council commissioner conference, or other major event; and

7) In consultation with the Scout executive / staff advisor, select and carry out a major project in the council.

Arrowhead Award Requirements for Assistant Council Commissioners (Administration):

1) Create a position description for the ACC role and obtain approval of the council commissioner;

2) Develop a work plan for your position that covers the program year;

3) Implement the work plan with continuous evaluation throughout the program year;

4) Report on work plan progress at council commissioner staff meetings;

5) Chair or actively take part in six council commissioner meetings;

6) Give leadership to a council commissioner conference or other major event; and

7) In consultation with the council Commissioner, select and carry out

a major project in the council, examples of Administrative AACs include AAC for: Commissioner Training and Recognition, Unit Health, New Unit Support, Administration, Commissioner Conference/College, Diversity, etc.

District Commissioner and Assistants:

1) Work with your district executive to evaluate all commissioners you supervise;

2) Achieve a ratio of one unit commissioner for every three units in the district or service area;

3) Develop and put into action a suitable recruiting plan;

4) Chair or take part actively in six district commissioner staff meetings;

5) Attend six district committee meetings (not required for assistants);

6) Attend a council commissioner conference, with a majority of your staff;

7) Provide personal coaching for the commissioners you supervise; and

8) Develop and implement a plan to track and hold your unit commissioner's accountable for monthly unit visits.

Unit Commissioner:

1) Visit each assigned unit eight or more times throughout the year;

2) Fill in and follow up on Commissioner Work Sheets or self-assessment forms for each assigned unit;

3) Conduct membership and leadership inventories in each assigned unit;

4) Attend six district commissioner staff meetings and provide the training topic for one meeting;

5) Participate in a charter review meeting that results in on-time unit re-registration;

6) Participate in a charter presentation;

7) Attend a council commissioner conference; and

8) Help a unit resolve a specific problem or improve some aspect of their unit operation.

Roundtable Commissioner:

1) Review all material in the Current *Venturing Program Forum Guide*, current *Boy Scout Leader Roundtable Planning Guide*, or current *Cub Scout Leader Roundtable Planning Guide*;

2) Review all material in *Troop Program Resources* and *Troop Program Features* or *Den & Pack Meeting Resource Guide*;

3) Recruit a roundtable staff;

4) Lead staff in preparing a one-year roundtable outline;

5) Supervise the staff in conducting these roundtables;

6) With the district commissioner and district executive, develop and use an attendance promotion plan; and

7) Attend a council commissioner conference, roundtable, or planning conference.

Commissioners assuming a new commissioner position are encouraged to complete the Arrowhead Honor projects for the new position.

Skipper's Key

Not current – issued 1947 ~ 1948.

This knot was worn by recipients of the Skipper's Key. It was presented to a Sea Scout Skipper that completed the tenure, training, and performance requirements that were published at that time. Requirements were similar to the then current Scoutmaster's Key.

Scouter's Award / Scouter's Training Award

Current – issued 2013 ~ present.

Change for color of both border and knot.

The award was called the Scouter's Award starting sometime after 1947 and by 1956 was changed back to Scouter's Training Award. The award is presented to any individual in Scouting (other than the key positions for the Scouter's Key) that has completed the tenure, training, and performance for the position they hold in Scouting.

The appropriate device(s) is/are worn on the knot to depict how the award was earned. Note – multiple devices may be worn to depict the various programs the award was issued for. Devices were first authorized in 1975 for the Scouter's Training Award and knot. Until 1974, this award was earned only once.

During the period of 1957 ~ 1969 the Scouter's Training Award knot was discontinued. During that period of time, recipients of the Scouter's Training Award wore the Scouter's Key knot without devices.

See requirements following the patches.

Current – issued 1998 ~ 2002 & 2004 ~ present.

Change for color of both border and knot.

Not current – issued 2002 ~ 2004.

Both color of knot and border changed.

Not current – issued 1983 ~ 1988.

Background color change to match a new uniform. This patch replaced the following patches.

Not current – issued 1947 ~ 1958 & 1969 ~ 1983.

Designed for wear on the Boy Scout uniform.

The knot was discontinued for use from 1958 until 1969. Scouter's would wear the Scouter's Key knot without a device for the Scouter's Training award during that time period.

Designed for wear on the Boy Scout uniform.

Not current – issued 1969 ~ 1979.

Designed for wear on the Explorer uniform.

Not current – issued 1969 ~ 1978.

Designed for wear on the Sea Explorer white uniform.

Not current – issued 1969 ~ 1979.

Designed for wear on the Sea Explorer blue and Cub Scout uniforms.

Cub Scouters (1947 ~ 1988), Explorer leaders, and Air Explorer leaders previously earned this award.

Current requirements for the Scouter's Training Award are as follows:

Scouter's Training Award Requirements Cub Scouting[30]

Tenure

Complete at least two years of tenure as a registered adult leader in the Cub Scout Pack.

Training

Do the following requirements:

- Complete basic training for any Cub Scout leader position.
- Complete *This is Scouting* training.
- Attend a Pow Wow or University of Scouting (or equivalent) or attend at least four roundtables (or equivalent) during each year of the tenure used for this award.

Performance

Do the following during the tenure used for this award:

- Participate in an annual pack planning meeting in each year.
- Serve as an adult leader in a pack that achieves at least the Bronze level of Journey to Excellence in each year. The Quality Unit

---

[30] Publication 511-057, 2012 Printing

Award is acceptable if the tenure used is prior to 2011.

- Give primary leadership in meeting at least one pack Journey to Excellence objective in each year.
- Participate in at least one additional supplemental or advanced training event at the council, area, region, or national level during the two years.

Scouter's Training Award Requirements for Boy Scouting[31]

Tenure

Complete at least two years of tenure as a registered adult leader in a Boy Scout troop.

Training

Do the following:

- Complete basic training for any Boy Scout leader position.
- Complete *This Is Scouting*.
- Attend a university of Scouting (or equivalent) or attend at least four roundtables (or equivalent) during each year of the tenure used for this award.

Performance

Do the following during the tenure used for this award:

- Participate in an annual troop planning meeting in each year.
- Serve as an adult leader in a troop that achieves at least the Bronze level of Journey to Excellence in each year. The Quality Unit Award is acceptable if the tenure used is prior to 2011.
- Give primary leadership in meeting at least on e troop Journey to Excellence objective in each year.
- Participate in at least one additional supplemental or advanced training event at either a council, area, region, or national level during the two years.

Scouter's Training Award for Varsity Scouting Requirements[32]

Tenure

Complete at least two years of tenure as a registered adult leader in a Varsity Scout team.

Training

Do the following:

---

[31] Publication 511-058, 2012 Printing
[32] Publication 511-059, 2012 Printing
[33] January 1, 2014 requirements. Refer to web site:
http://www.scouting.org/filestore/training/pdf/Sea_Scout_Adult_Training_Award.pdf
[34] Publication 511-060, 2012 Printing
[35] *www.scouting.org/training/adult.aspx*, District Committee Training Award

- Complete basic training for Varsity Scout Leaders.

- Complete *This Is Scouting*.

- Attend a university of Scouting (or equivalent) or attend at least four roundtables/huddles (or equivalent) during each year of the tenure used for this award.

Performance

Do the following during the tenure used for this award:

- Participate in an annual team planning meeting in each year.

- Serve as an adult leader in a troop that achieves at least the Bronze level of Journey to Excellence in each year. The Quality Unit Award is acceptable if the tenure used is prior to 2011.

- Give primary leadership in meeting at least one team Journey to Excellence objective in each year. Participate actively in three team parents' nights or courts of honor.

- Participate in at least one additional supplemental or advanced training event at either a council, area, region, or national level during the two years.

- Serve for at least one year as team committee person assigned to one of the five program fields of emphasis.

Sea Scouting Adult Training Award Requirements[33]

Mates and ship committee members earn this award by qualifying for the requirements listed below.

Training

Complete *Venturing Leader Youth Protection.*

Complete *Sea Scouting Adult Leader Basic Training.*

Complete boating safety course offered by the U.S. Coast Guard Auxiliary, U.S. Power Squadron, or NASBLA approved boater safety course.

Tenure

Complete two years of registered tenure in any adult capacity in Sea Scouts.

Performance

1. Participate in ILSS training or the quarterdeck training for the ship in each year.

2. Serve as an adult leader in a ship that achieves at least bronze level of Journey to Excellence in each year.

3. Give primary leadership in meeting at least one ship Journey to Excellence objective in each year.

4. Participate in at least on e additional supplemental or advanced training event at the council, area, region, or national level during the two years.

5. Perform to the satisfaction of the Skipper your assigned leadership duties.

Certification

The Skipper and Commissioner must approve all applications.

Venturing Training Award Requirements[34]

Tenure

Complete at least two years of tenure as a registered adult leader in a Venturing crew.

Training

Do the following:

- Complete basic training for any Venturing leader position
- Complete *This is Scouting* training.
- Attend a university of Scouting (or equivalent) or attend at least four roundtables/teen leader's council meetings/ Venturing officers association meetings (or equivalent) during each year of the tenure used for this award.

Performance

Do the following during the tenure for this award:

- Participate in an annual crew planning meeting in each year.
- Serve as an adult leader in a crew that achieves at least the Bronze level of Journey to Excellence in each year. The Quality Unit Award is acceptable if the tenure used is prior to 2011.
- Give primary leadership in meeting at least one crew Journey to Excellence objective in each year.
- Participate in at least one additional supplemental or advanced training event at either a council, area, region, or national level during the two years.

Roundtable Staff Training Award Requirements

Training

Review with the roundtable commissioner orientation material in the current *Cub Scout Leader Roundtable Planning Guide, Boy Scout Leader Roundtable Planning Guide*, or *Venturing Program Forum Guide*.

Review all material in the current *Den & Pack Meeting Resource Guide/Webelos Leader Guide, Troop Program Resources,* and *Troop Program Features,* or *Varsity Scout Game Plan*.

Complete basic training for Cub Scout, Boy Scout, or Venturing roundtable commissioners and staff.

Tenure

Complete two years as a roundtable staff member.

Performance

Do the following:

- Participate in six roundtable staff meetings.

- Actively assist in six roundtables.

- Conduct a successful roundtable attendance promotion project.

- Conduct a pre-opening actively and an opening ceremony.

- Conduct or be responsible for a major project, presentation, or demonstration at one roundtable.

District Committee Scouter's Training Award Requirements[35]

Tenure

Complete at least two years of registered tenure as a member of a district committee.

Training

Do the following during the tenure for this award:

- Attend a District Committee Training Workshop.

- Review *The District* manual and discuss your role with your operating committee chair, district chair, or district executive.

- Complete *This is Scouting* training.

Performance

Do the following during the tenure for this award:

- Take part actively in at least six district committee meetings.

- Be a member of an operating committee that meets at least the Bronze level in a related Journey to Excellence objective in each year used for tenure.

- Participate in at least one additional supplemental or advanced training event at the council, area, region, or national level.

- Conduct or be responsible for a major project, presentation, or demonstration at one roundtable.

Professional Training Award

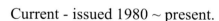

Current - issued 1980 ~ present.

Material knot is embroidered on was changed from white to black.

Professional Circle

The professional circle is presented to professional Scouters for completion of the professional training program, tenure, and performance. [36]

Tenure

Professional tenure of at least four years.

Training

Successfully attend all three sessions of the Professional Executive

---

[36] Information provided by the Professional Development Division

Institute (PEI).

Performance

Completion of any three of the following advanced courses:

    a. People Management – Part I.

    b. People Management – Part II.

    c. People Management – Part III.

    d. Wood Badge or National Camping School (Must be taken during professional tenure).

    e. Any BSA course(s), including but not limited to, those through the Professional Development Division, Finance Division, or Philmont Training Center.

    f. One non-BSA course that is job related, consisting of at least 15 classroom hours, taken during professional tenure.

    Note: All courses must be taken during professional tenure.

        Courses that do not qualify include, but are not limited to: area, regional, national conferences, direct service workshops (except where they exceed 15 hours), or council in-service training or training intended primarily for youth or volunteers (other than those listed above).

Fellowship Honor

This award may be earned by completing the following requirements:

1. Complete the requirements for and be awarded the professional circle.

2. Complete two additional courses beyond the three required for the professional circle.

3. Receive prior approval of a fellowship thesis based on council, district, or division operations problems with a detailed resolution of the problem. This must be reviewed and accepted by the council executive and the professional development division.

Recipients wear the Boy Scout device on the Professional Training Award knot (see devices in this book). This is a rare award.

Not current – Issued 1980.

This knot was first produced on white material. National staff did not like the outer white border, and had all future knots produced on black cloth.

Seabadge

Not current – issued 2004 ~ 2011.

Both the color and shape of the trident were changed.

This award was discontinued in 2011, but may be worn if earned prior to the date discontinued. This was presented to Sea Scout leaders who completed the Sea Badge class. Originally attendees of Sea Badge also needed to complete a ticket, similar to Wood Badge that took between 8 and 24

months. The ticket was re-established for the Sea Badge program in 2011.

Not current – issued 1999 ~ 2004.

Both the color and shape of the trident were changed.

Not current – issued 1988 ~ 1999.

Unit Leader Award of Merit

Current – issued 2010 ~ present

The Unit Leader Award of Merit replaces the Scoutmaster, Varsity Team Coach, and Venturing Crew Advisor award of merit programs. This new recognition has revised requirements and may be earned by Cubmasters as well.

Note: Skippers are not eligible for this award.

Requirements

The nominee must:

1. Be currently registered Cubmaster, Scoutmaster, Coach, or Advisor who has served in that position at least 18 continuous months.
2. Meet the training requirements for the registered position.
3. Distribute a printed or electronic annual unit program plan and calendar to each family in the unit.
4. Effectively use the advancement method so that at least 60 percent of the unit's youth have advanced at least once during the last 12 months.
5. Cultivate a positive relationship with the chartered organization.
6. Project a positive image of Scouting in the community.

Nomination Procedure

1. The unit committee chair completes the Unit Leader Award of Merit Nomination Form on behalf of the unit committee. For Boy Scout troops, Varsity Scout teams, and Venturing crews, the nomination must include endorsement by the Senior Patrol Leader, Team Captain, or Crew President, respectively.
2. The unit or district commissioner certifies that the form is complete.
3. The unit submits the nomination form to the council for approval by the Scout Executive and Council Commissioner or President.

The Award

Upon receipt of the approved nomination form, the council may present the Unit Leader Award of Merit, which includes a certification, square knot with the appropriate device, and a special unit leader emblem.

Recognition of this achievement may be presented at appropriate district or council events, such as a district or council leader recognition dinners, training events, and board meetings.

Alumni Knot Award

Current – issued 2011 ~ present.

Complete the Application for the Alumni Knot Award and submit the application to the National Alumni Task Force for approval.

Applicants must be currently registered adult Scouters of the Boy Scouts of America.

All applicants must receive the approval of their local council's alumni relations committee chairperson and their council Scout executive.

Area I – Alumni Identification/Promotion *(Complete any 3 of the 5 requirements in this section)*

- Create and distribute a communications vehicle designed to identify unregistered alumni, that has been approved by the local council alumni committee staff advisor.

- Assist in planning an alumni activity at the district, council, community, region or national level.

- Make contact with at least 5 adult alumni, not currently registered with the BSA, engage them in a serious discussion about the Scouting program, provide them each with an Alumni Connection card and follow-up to see if they have visited the web site.

- Make two presentations to non-Scout groups promoting the BSA, alumni membership and volunteering (Alumni specific speech draft/template).

- Obtain at least two scout profiles or stories, use them in local council alumni promotion and forward a copy of the profiles/stories to the national alumni office.

Area II – Alumni Engagement *(Complete all 4 of the requirements in this section)*

- Make arrangements for at least two unregistered alumni to attend a Scout activity at the district, council, community, region or national level *(must be different than those used below in this section)*.

- Facilitate at least two alumni becoming registered members of the BSA *(must be different than those used above in this section)*.

- Personally solicit and obtain Friends of Scouting gifts from at least two unregistered alumni *(must be different than those used above in this section)*.

- Recruit at least two unregistered alumni to volunteer at a district, council, community, region or national event *(must be different than those used above in this section)*.

Area III – Personal Participation (*Complete all four of the requirements below in this section*)

- Serve on a local council or national alumni or National Eagle Scout Association committee for at least one year.

- Visit the Alumni Connection web site and complete the alumni scavenger hunt.

- Upload two of your own Scouting-related photos to the Alumni Scrapbook section of the Alumni web site.

- Share your favorite Scouting memory through the Rekindle Memories section of the alumni web site and send an e-card to at least five unregistered alumni.

All Eagle Scouts must complete one additional requirement in this section:

- Become a member of the National Eagle Scout Association and register on the NESA web site.

Area IV – Personal Education (*Complete any 1 of the 3 requirements in this section*)

- Become an Alumni Ambassador by successfully completing the online alumni volunteer training.

- Attend an alumni session at the BSA National meeting.

- Attend an alumni course at the Philmont Training Center.

Den Mother's Training Award / Den Leader's Training Award

Not current – issued 1975 ~ 1988.

This award was discontinued December 31, 1988, but may be worn if earned. This was presented to Den Leaders (originally called Den Mother's) in a Cub Scout pack upon completion of required tenure, training, and performance requirements.

Den Leader Coach's Training Award

Not current – issued 1975 ~ 1988.

This award was discontinued December 31, 1988, but may be worn if earned. This was presented to Den Leader Coach's in a Cub Scout pack upon completion of required tenure, training, and performance requirements. This knot was re-named as the Cub Scouter Award.

Cubmaster Award

Not current – issued 1988 ~ 2012.

This award was discontinued in 2012, but may be worn if earned. Awarded to Cubmasters upon completion of required tenure, training, and performance requirements.

Webelos Den Leader Award

Not current – issued 1988 ~ 2012.

This award was discontinued in 2012, but may be worn if earned.

Awarded to Webelos Den Leaders upon completion of required tenure, training, and performance requirements.

Den Leader Award / Cub Scout Den Leader Award/ Den Leader Training Award

Current – issued 1988 ~ 2001 as the Den Leader award, and 2001 ~ 2012 as the Cub Scout Den Leader award, and 2012 ~ present as the Den Leader Training Award.

The way to recognize this award from the previous award is this knot is on a plain weave, while the original Den Leader award was on a twill material.

This award may be earned 3 times:

- Tiger Cub Den Leader
- Cub Scout Den Leader (Wolf and Bear)
- Webelos Den Leader

A device is worn to represent which award(s) was/were earned.

Awarded to Cub Scout Den Leaders that have completed the following requirements: [37]

Tenure

Complete one year as a registered den leader in the position selected (Tiger Cub den leader, Wolf Cub Scout den leader, Bear Cub Scout den leader, or Webelos den leader). Tiger Cub den leader's tenure can be the program year as long as it is greater than eight months.

Training

Complete the basic training for the selected den leader position.

Complete *This Is Scouting* training.

Attend a Pow Wow or University of Scouting (or equivalent), or attend at least four roundtables (or equivalent) during the tenure used for this award.

Performance

Do **five** of the following during the tenure used for this award:

- Have an assistant den leader who meets regularly with your den.
- Have a den chief who meets regularly with your den.
- Graduate at least 70% of your den into the next level.
- Take leadership in planning and conducting a den service project.

---

[37] Publication 511-052, 2012 Printing

- Have a published den meeting/activity schedule for the den's parents.
- Participate with your den in a Cub Scout day camp or resident camp.
- Complete *Basic Adult Leader Outdoor Orientation* (BALOO).
- Complete *Outdoor Leadership Skills for Webelos Leaders.*
- Participate with your den in at least one family camp; if your den is a Webelos den, participate with your den in at least two overnight camps.
- Take leadership in planning two den outdoor activities.
- Hold monthly den meeting and den activity planning sessions with your assistant den leaders.

Den Leader Coach Award

Not current – issued 1988 ~ 2001.

There have been numerous shades of blue used for the knot and border over the years.

This award was discontinued in 2001, but may be worn if earned. This was presented to a Den Leader Coach in a Cub Scout pack upon completion of required tenure, training, and performance requirements.

Pack Trainer Award

Not current – issued 2008 ~ 2012.

This award was discontinued in 2012, but may be worn if earned. This was presented to Pack Trainers in a Cub Scout pack upon completion of required tenure, training, and performance.

Not current – issued 2006.

National Supply issued this knot without National Office approval. A recall was then issued and requested that all knots sold be turned in and sent back to Supply Division for destruction.

Cub Scouter Award

Not current – issued 1988 ~ 2012.

This is nearly the same knot that was previously issued for the Den Leader Coach's Training Award. This one has a slightly lighter blue boarder and is on a plain weave material instead of a twill material.

This award was discontinued in 2012, but may be worn if earned. This was presented to registered Cub Scout Leaders upon completion of required tenure, training, and performance.

Tiger Cub Group Coach Award /
Tiger Cub Coach Award /
Tiger Cub Den Leader Award

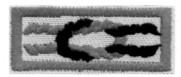

Not current – issued 1993 ~ 1998 as the Tiger Cub Group Coach award, then 1998 ~ 2001 as the Tiger Cub Coach award, and finally 2001 ~ 2012 as the Tiger Cub Den Leader award.

This award was discontinued in 2012, but may be worn if earned while the award was current.

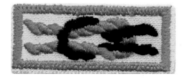

Not current – issued 1994 ~ 1995 time period.

Scoutmaster Award of Merit /
Venturing Advisor Award of Merit /
Varsity Team Coach Award of Merit

Not current – issued 2002 ~ 2009.

Border and background color change.

This award was discontinued in 2009, but may be worn if earned.

This knot was replaced by the Unit Leader Award of Merit effective November 2009, although the new knot was not available unit January 2010.

Note: The Venturing Advisor Award of Merit started in 1998.

Not current – issued 1996 ~ 2002.

Border and background color change to match a new uniform.

Not current – issued 1987 ~ 1996.

International Scouter's Award

Current – 2013 ~ present.

Misprint. Note the purple over loop. White is never the dominate color. The over loop should be white.

Award was created in February 2003 to encourage Scouters to broaden their involvement in Scouting through participation in world Scouting activities and to recognize those Scouters for their contributions to world Scouting. [38]

Requirements:

Complete any six of the following, from at least three of the following categories:

---

[38] Requirements from the International Division, Boy Scouts of America, publication 22-721, 2002 Printing

I. Giving leadership to international Scouting:

- Serve as council international representative, council international committee member, or BSA International Committee member for a minimum of three consecutive years.

- Serve as a registered adult leader with a Direct Service Cub Scout Pack, Boy Scout troop, or Venturing crew.

- Serve at least one year in any international Scouting position approved by the BSA International Division.

II. Giving leadership to international events held in the United States:

- Host Scouts/Scouters (minimum of three visitors per group) from another country as part of an official national, council, district, or unit activity.

- Serve on the international staff at a national Scout jamboree.

- Assist in the organization of your council's participation in international Camp Staff program. Be responsible for bringing a foreign Scout on staff to the council's summer camp program for two summer camp seasons.

III. Giving leadership to international events held in other countries:

- Serve as an adult leader in a BSA contingent to a world Scout jamboree or Pan-American Scout jamboree.

- Serve as an adult leader for a group of BSA Scouts participating in an event held by a foreign Scout association recognized by the World Organization of the Scout Movement. The activity may be an exchange program, camp experience, tour activity, or home hospitality function.

- Serve on the international service staff of a world Scout jamboree.

IV. Educating self and other:

- Attend an international Scout conference at the Philmont Training Center. Share what you have learned with others in your council.

- Promote international Scouting at a district, council, regional, or national event.

- Participate in organizing or providing leadership for a BSA Scout activity in another country what involves interaction with Scouts from that country, such as an exchange program, camping experience, or tour activity.

V. Giving support to international Scouting:

- Organize a collection for the World Friendship Fund at two district and/or council events.
- Become a recruit member of the Order of the Condor for the Interamerican Scout Foundation.
- Become or recruit a Baden-Powell Fellow for the World Scout Foundation.

Not current – 2003 ~ 2013.

James E. West Fellowship Award

Current – issued 1993 ~ present.

The James West Fellowship Program is probably the one award that sparks the most misunderstanding when spotted on a uniform. Some folks immediately assume that the award was simply purchased, which is not accurate.

Encouraging gifts to BSA local council endowment funds is one of Scouting's highest priorities. It is one of the best ways to ensure that your council can continue to offer the outstanding programs it now has and also grow to meet the need of the youth and communities it serves.

In its gratitude for such support, the BSA nationally offers three distinct endowment recognition awards. These awards are presented by local councils to donors who support Scouting's financial future with council endowment gifts. These programs are: [39]

The James E. West Fellowship Program

James E. West was the first Chief Scout Executive of the Boy Scouts of America, and he served in that position for more than three decades. The West Fellowship award had been available for gifts of $1,000 and up in cash or marketable securities to a council endowment fund.

In 2012 the program changed to award for gifts of $1,000+ (Bronze Member Level), $5,000+ (Silver Member Level), $10,000+ (Gold Member Level) and $15,000+ (Diamond Member Level). The gift must be in addition to – and not replace or diminish – the donor's annual Friends of Scouting support. Many individuals and corporations make these gifts on behalf of someone else – such as an Eagle Scout, Silver Beaver recipient, a retirement, a special accomplishment, or anniversary – or in memory of a special individual.

Individuals wear the James E. West Fellowship Knot.

For more information about the James E. West Fellowship program, contact your local council or Finance Impact (BSA National) @ 972-580-2000.

The 1910 Society (Discontinued in 2012)

Founded in 1910, the Boy Scouts of America has grown into something larger and more significant than anyone anticipated. The Boy Scouts honor that special date by presenting the 1910 Society award to donors who make gifts of $25,000 or more, outright or in a pledge payable within 5 years, to a local council/national operating, capital, and/or endowment fund. These gifts can be in the form of cash, securities, land, five-year pledges, or other property suitable for a council/national endowment fund or easily converted

---

[39] National Recognition of Local Council Endowment Support, Boy Scout of America guide, web site: *www.scouting.org/filestore/pdf/Major_Gifts_Recognition_brochure.pdf*.

to cash. There are six levels of recognition (divided into four areas) in the 1910 Society that honor four very special individuals who shaped modern-day Scouting:

1. **Ernest Thompson Seton**, nationally known artist and naturalist, author of the first official American Scout handbook and many other books important to Scouting:

   Seton Level: $25,000 minimum gift

2. **Daniel Carter Beard**, first chairman of the National Court of Honor, national Scout commissioner, and author of many well-known books and stories for youth:

   Beard Level: $100,000 minimum gift

3. **Theodore Roosevelt**, first Chief Scout Citizen, first vice president of the BSA, and president of the United States:

   Roosevelt Level: $500,000 minimum gift

4. **Waite Phillips**, one of the BSA's first benefactors, and donor to the BSA of almost 130,000 acres of land in New Mexico which became Philmont Scout Ranch:

   Phillips Level: $1,000,000 minimum gift
   Phillips Silver Level: $5,000,000 minimum gift
   Phillips Gold Level: $10,000,000 minimum gift

Individuals wear the Endowment Recognition Knot with a 1910 Society device (see device on page 57). **Note**: This device is no longer current.

The Founders Circle (Discontinued in 2012)

The newest level of endowment recognition, the Founders Circle, is intended to recognize a gift of $100,000.00 or more in the form of a deferred gift commitment to a local council operating, capital, and/or endowment fund. With deferred giving (also called planned giving) so widely and effectively used by so many donors, the BSA wants to recognize the importance of such major gifts. Unlike the other endowment recognition awards, a donor may qualify for membership with gifts made through:

- Charitable bequests in a will or codicil;

- Charitable trusts, such as unitrusts, annuity trusts, and lead trusts;

- BSA Gift Annuities or BSA Pooled Income Fund gifts;

- Life insurance/retirement plan designations; and/or
- Other deferred gifts approved by the local council.

There are four levels of membership within the Founders Circle. They are:

1. **Bronze** - $100,000 minimum gift commitment.

2. **Silver** - $250,000 minimum gift commitment.

3. **Gold** - $500,000 minimum gift commitment.

4. **Platinum** - $1,000,000 minimum gift commitment.

Individuals wear the Endowment Recognition Knot with a Founders Circle device (see page 57). **Note**: This device is no longer current.

Note: Only registered Scouters or youth members receive and wear the square knot.

Second Century Society

In 2012 the Second Century Society was introduced. An outright gift of $25,000 or more, payable over five years, or a deferred gift of $100,000 or more, to a local council, BSA Foundation, High-adventure base, or any BSA entity for operating, capital, or endowment.

There are four member levels: $25,000, $100,000, $500,000, and $1,000,000.

Members making outright gifts of $100,000 or more are designated as "Members with Distinction." Donors making deferred gifts of $500,000 or more are designated as "Legacy Members." Members in these categories receive special recognition and opportunities provided by the BSA Foundation.

Presidents Leadership Council

Gifts to or through the BSA Foundation payable over five years, as part of an advised fund, designated fund, trust, or other foundation fund structure. Gifts may be designated to benefit local councils, high-adventure facilities, or other BSA entities.

There are 3 levels of the Presidents Leadership Council: $1,000,000+, $5,000,000+ and $10,000,000+.

For more information about the Second Century Society and Presidents Leadership Council, contact the National Foundation @ 972-580-2219.

Order of the Arrow Legacy Fellowship

A device is worn on the knot for gifts to the National Order of the Arrow program of $1,000.00 or more, in addition to the normal amount donated through their council Friends of Scouting campaign. See device on page 59.

National Eagle Scout Association Legacy Society

A device is worn on the knot for gifts to the National Eagle Scout Association of $1,000.00 or more, in addition to the normal amount donated through their council Friends of Scouting campaign. See device on page 59.

Devices for Knot Awards

Cub Scout

 Current – issued 1957 ~ present.

Worn on the following knot awards:

Scouter's Key

When earned as a Cubmaster prior to December 31, 1988 and June 1, 2012 ~ present.

Scouter's Training Award

Starting in 1975 ~ December 31, 1988 and June 1, 2012 ~ to present when earned in any capacity in the Cub Scout program except Den Leaders.

Starting in 1996 when earned as a member of the Cut Scout Roundtable Staff.

Religious Emblem (Youth)

Starting in 1983 for first-level emblem earned as a Tiger Cub or Cub Scout.

William D Boyce New-Unit Organizer Award

Starting in 2005 for second through forth award. Worn to depict the type of unit organized. More than one of these devices may be worn.

Unit Leader Award of Merit

2010 ~ present when awarded to a Cubmaster.

Den Leader Award

June 1, 2012 ~ to present when earned in by a Wolf and/or Bear Den Leader in the Cub Scout program.

Boy Scout

 Current – issued 1957 ~ present.

Worn on the following knot awards:

Scouter's Key

When earned as a Scoutmaster.

Scouter's Training Award

Starting in 1975 when earned in any capacity in the Boy Scout program.

Starting in 1996 when earned as a member of the Boy Scout Roundtable Staff.

Religious Emblem (Youth)

Starting in 1983 for emblem earned as a Boy Scout.

Scoutmaster/Venturing Advisor/Varsity Team Coach Award of Merit

Prior to 2010 when earned as a Scoutmaster.

Professional Training Award

Represents earning the Fellowship Honor.

William D Boyce New-Unit Organizer Award

Starting in 2005 for second through forth award. Worn to depict the type of unit organized. More than one of these devices may be worn.

Unit Leader Award of Merit

2010 ~ present when awarded to a Scoutmaster.

Exploring [CAW (Compass, Anchor, Wings)]

Not current – issued 1957 ~ 1958.

This is the original Exploring device.

Worn on the following knot award:

Scouter's Key

When earned as an Explorer Advisor.

Commissioner

Current – issued 1998 ~ present.

Design change from the 1st class emblem with wreath to universal emblem (tenderfoot emblem) with wreath.

Worn on the following knot awards:

Scouter's Key

When earned in the commissioner service.

Scouter's Training Award

When earned as Roundtable Staff through 1995.

Commissioner Award of Excellence in Unit Service

For the 2nd and 3rd times this award is earned.

Not current – issued 1957 ~ 1998.

Note the 1st class emblem in the center of the wreath.

Exploring (Circle V)

Not current – issued 1958 ~ 1969. This is the second Exploring device issued.

Worn on the following knot award:

Scouter's Key

When earned as an Explorer Advisor.

Air Explorer

Not current – issued 1958 ~ 1965.

Worn on the following knot award:

Scouter's Key

When earned as an Air Explorer Advisor.

Sea Explorer/Scout

Current – issued 1958 ~ present.

Worn on the following knot awards:

Scouter's Key

When earned as a Skipper. Also worn on the Scouter's Key when awarded the Skippers Key.

Scouter's Training Award

Starting in 1975 when earned in any capacity in the Sea Explorer/Scout program.

Distinguished Eagle Scout

Current – issued 1999 ~ present.

Design change in the shape of eagle and addition of the letters "BSA" on the device.

The Distinguished Eagle Scout Award was established in 1969 to acknowledge Eagle Scouts who have received extraordinary national level recognition, fame, or eminence within their field or avocation and have a strong record of voluntary service to their community. The recipient must have attained the Eagle Scout rank a minimum of 25 years before his nomination.

Worn on the following knot awards:

Eagle Scout Award

Eagle Scout NESA Life Membership Award

Not current – issued 1997 ~ 1998.

Not current – issued 1969 ~ 1997.

Exploring (Big E)

Not current – issued 1969 ~ 1998. This is the third and last Exploring device.

Worn on the following knot awards:

Scouter's Key

When earned as an Explorer Advisor.

Scouter's Training Award

Starting in 1975 when earned in any capacity in the Exploring program.

Religious Emblem (Youth)

Starting in 1983 for emblem earned as an Explorer, older Boy Scout or Varsity Scout.

Varsity Scout

Current – issued 1985 ~ present.

Worn on the following knot awards:

Scouter's Key

When earned as a Varsity Scout Coach.

Scouter's Training Award

When earned in any capacity in the Varsity Scout program.

Scoutmaster/Venturing Advisor/Varsity Team Coach Award of Merit

Prior to 2010 when presented to a Varsity Team Coach.

William D Boyce New-Unit Organizer Award

Starting in 2005 for second through forth award. Worn to depict the type of unit organized. More than one of these devices may be worn.

Unit Leader Award of Merit

2010 ~ present when awarded to a Team Coach.

Webelos

 Current – issued 1989 ~ present.

Worn on the following knot award:

Religious Emblem (Youth)

For emblem earned as a Webelos Scout.

Den Leader Award

June 1, 2012 ~ to present when earned in by a Webelos Den Leader in the Cub Scout program.

District Committee

 Current – issued 1993 ~ present.

Worn on the following knot award:

Scouter's Key

When earned as a member of the District Committee.

 Not current – issued 1993.

Note the 1st class emblem in the center.

Venturing

 Current – issued 1998 ~ present.

Worn on the following knot awards:

Scouter's Key

When earned as a Venturing Advisor.

Scouter's Training Award

When earned in any capacity in the Venturing program.

Religious Emblem (Youth)

For emblem earned as a Venturer, older Boy Scout or Varsity Scout.

Scoutmaster/Venturing Advisor Award of Merit

Prior to 2010 when presented to a Venturing Advisor or Skipper.

William D Boyce New-Unit Organizer Award

Starting in 2005 for second through forth award. Worn to depict the type of unit organized. More than one of these devices may be worn.

Unit Leader Award of Merit

2010 ~ when awarded to a Venturing Advisor.

1910 Society

Not current – issued 2000 ~ 2011.

Worn on the following knot award:

James E. West Fellowship Award

Represents donations meeting the 1910 Society requirements.

Founders Circle

Not current – issued 2000 ~ 2011.

Worn on the following knot award:

James E. West Fellowship Award

Represents donations meeting the Founders Circle requirements.

Philmont Training Center Masters Track

Current – issued 2009 ~ present.

Worn on the following knot award:

Philmont Training Center Masters Track Knot

Represents completion of the 3rd Track.

The Glenn A. & Melinda W. Adams National Eagle Scout Service Project of the Year Award - Council Level

Current – issued 2011 ~ present.

This award is a National award upon recommendation of, and presented by Council.

Each council that has an active National Eagle Scout Association (NESA) chapter in their council may present the best Eagle Scout project to national council for a council recommended award. Each Council, with an active NESA committee my select one project as the best for their council and forward that recommendation to National.

The device may be worn on one of the following knots. Only one of these knots may be worn on a uniform at any one time.

Worn on the following knot awards:

Eagle Scout Award

Eagle Scout NESA Life Membership Award

The Glenn A. & Melinda W. Adams National Eagle Scout Service Project of the Year Award - Region Level

Current – issued 2011 ~ present.

This award is a National award upon recommendation of, and presented by Region.

National Council will send all Council level awards to the appropriate Region for selection by

Region for the most outstanding Eagle Scout project within their Region.

Each Region selects the most outstanding Eagle service project of the year from those sent to National by the Councils within their respective Region. Each Region may recommend up to 1 award per year. A $500.00 award is presented to the Scout who's project is selected, and a matching amount is presented to the Scout's Council.

Worn on the following knot awards:

Eagle Scout Award

Eagle Scout NESA Life Membership Award

The Glenn A. & Melinda W. Adams National Eagle Scout Service Project of the Year Award - National Level

Current – issued 2011 ~ present.

This award is a National award upon recommendation of, and presented by National.

National will select the most outstanding project from those selected by the Regions. A $2,500.00 award is presented to the Scout who's project is selected, and a matching amount is presented to the Scout's Council.

Only one of the three Adams awards may be presented to any one individual. Therefore if a scout is presented the National (Silver) award, then he does not receive the Region (Gold) or Council (Bronze) award.

Worn on the following knot awards:

Eagle Scout Award

Eagle Scout NESA Life Membership Award

NESA Outstanding Eagle Scout Award

Current – issued 2012 ~ present.

The NESA Outstanding Eagle Scout Award (NOESA) is a prestigious recognition granted by the local council's NESA committee to Eagle Scouts who have demonstrated outstanding achievement at the local, state, or regional level. Unlike the Distinguished Eagle Scout Award, which is a national award, the NOESA recognizes Eagle Scouts whose efforts have made a positive impact closer to home.

The award may only be approval by the local NESA committee who forwards the application to the National Eagle Scout Association for verification and award completion. This award is issued on the basis of 2 for first 100 Eagle Scouts awarded in their council in the prior year and 1 for each additional 100 Eagles. A council may approve up to 199 NOESA awards per year using that ratio. A NOESA award may not be presented to an individual who has the Distinguished Eagle Scout Award (DESA).

Worn on the following knot awards:

Eagle Scout Award

Eagle Scout NESA Life Membership Award

Not current – issued 2011 ~ 2012.

This device was originally designed prior to the medal being designed. It was later determined that the device should be the same style as the medal.

Order of the Arrow Legacy Fellowship

Current – issued 2011 ~ present.

The OA Legacy Fellowship is presented to Arrowman who donate $1,000.00 to the National Order of the Arrow Endowment program.

The Legacy Fellowship is the first opportunity for Order of the Arrow members to make a direct contribution to the national OA endowment, furthering their support of Scouting. The national OA endowment provides direct funding of Lodge Service Grants, Josh R. Sain Memorial Scholarships, OA High Adventure, major conservation projects like *Arrowcorps* and SummitCorps, and continuing support of youth leaders.

The donor must first be a James E. West Fellow prior to donating to the National OA Endowment. All contributions to the national OA endowment should be in addition to the regular support of the contributor's regular support of their council's fundraising programs.

Worn on the following knot award:

James E. West Fellowship

Tiger Cub Den Leader

Current – issued 2012 ~ present.

Worn on the following knot award:

Den Leader Award

Effective June 1, 2012 when earned by a Tiger Cub Den Leader in the Cub Scout program.

National Eagle Scout Association Legacy Society

Current – issued 2013 ~ present.

The National Eagle Scout Association (NESA) Legacy Society is the first opportunity to make a direct contribution to NESA endowment furthering the support of Scouting. The NESA endowment provides direct funding of Eagle Scout scholarships, NESA committee service grants, and career networking and encouragement for all Scouts who wear the Eagle Scout badge.

Fellowship in the NESA Legacy Society is open to any currently registered youth or adult Scouter who has been recognized as a James E. West Fellow. All contributions should be in addition to the regular support of the contributor's regular support of their council's fundraising programs.

Worn on the following knot award:

James E. West Fellowship

Eagle Palms

Eagle palms were never designed as devices for knots. They are however authorized for wear on the Eagle Scout knot and the National Eagle Scout Association (NESA) Life Member knot. Only one of those two knots may be worn at any one time.

Eagle Scout Palms were first announced in the 1926 Annual Report on page 59, which read:

"Palms will be awarded for additional merit badges earned to the Eagle Scout who presents to the local court of honor or the examining committee in such form as it may determine, satisfactory definite and concrete evidence that has met the following requirements:

1. That he has continued to put into practice the ideals & principles of the Scout Oath and Law, the motto "Be Prepared" and the daily good turn.

2. The he has maintained an active service relationship to Scouting.

3. That he has made an effort to develop and demonstrate leadership ability.

For five merit badges earned in addition to the 21 required for Eagle Scout rank, the scout is entitled to wear a bronze palm: for 10 badges he is entitled to wear a gold palm; for 15 badges, a silver palm; a combination of palms may be used to indicate merit badges in excess of 15."

It should be noted that between June 1972 and July 1979, 24 merit badges were required for the rank of Eagle Scout. Palms were still 5, 10 and 15 beyond the Eagle Scout rank to earn the palms.

A combination of bronze, gold, and silver palms may be worn based on the total number of palms earned (i.e.: for 25 additional merit badges, wear one silver and one gold palm).

Eagle palms were originally manufactured with a spin Latch on the back. Shortly after the start of World War II, a crude clutch was used. This was needed to reduce the production time and expense. After the war was over the spin lock was again used until shortly after 1958. After that a short stem was used on the palms. Starting in 1969 a long stem was used. During the 1970s manufacturing started to use a medium stem. It was not until after the turn of the 21st century that the long stem was again used.

Bronze Palm

Current – issued 1942 ~ present.

This basic design was introduced shortly after the start of World War II.

Worn on the following knot awards:

Eagle Scout Award

Eagle Scout NESA Life Membership Award

Presented for five additional merit badges earned in excess of the required number needed for the Eagle Scout award.

Not current – issued 1926 ~ 1942.

Gold Palm

Current – issued 1942 ~ present.

Worn on the following knot awards:

Eagle Scout Award

Eagle Scout NESA Life Membership Award

Presented for ten additional merit badges earned in excess of the required number needed for the Eagle Scout award.

 Not current – issued 1926 ~ 1942.

Silver Palm

 Current – issued 1942 ~ present.

Worn on the following knot awards:

Eagle Scout Award

Eagle Scout NESA Life Membership Award

Presented for fifteen additional merit badges earned in excess of the required number needed for the Eagle Scout award.

 Not current – issued 1926 ~ 1942.

Listing of Knot Issues[40]

A. For Bravery

Nmbr	Insignia	Bkgd	Fab	Emb	Tp	Right	Left	Border	CB	GB	PB	GP	LO	LG	WP	WL	LO1	FDL	Misc
K-A01a	Honor Medal	KHA	CTL	Sw	1	RED	RED	BRN	[ ]										
K-A01b	Honor Medal	KHA	CTL	Sw	1	LRD	LRD	BRN	[ ]										
K-A01c	Honor Medal	LKH	FTR	Sw	1	DRD	DRD	BRN		[ ]									
K-A01d	Honor Medal	LKH	FTR	Sw	1	CAR	CAR	BRN		[ ]									
K-A01e	Honor Medal	LKH	FTR	Sw	1	CAR	CAR	MBN		[ ]									Thin Knot
K-A01f	Honor Medal	LKH	FTR	Sw	1	RED	RED	MBN											[ ] BLU PB
K-A01g	Honor Medal	LKH	FTR	Sw	1	LRD	LRD	MBN											[ ] BLU PB
K-A01h	Honor Medal	LKH	FTR	Sw	1	LRD	LRD	LBN											[ ] BLU PB
K-A01i	Honor Medal	LKH	FTL	Sw	1	LRD	LRD	BRN				[ ]							
K-A01j	Honor Medal	LKH	FTL	Sw	1	RED	RED	MBN					[ ]						
K-A01k	Honor Medal	LKH	FTL	Sw	1	LRD	LRD	MBN				[ ]							
K-A01l	Honor Medal	LKH	FTL	Sw	1	DPR	DPR	LBN				[ ]							
K-A01m	Honor Medal	LKH	FTL	Sw	1	DRD	DRD	LBN				[ ]							Thin Knot
K-A01n	Honor Medal	LKH	FTL	Sw	1	RED	RED	LBN				[ ]							
K-A01o	Honor Medal	BGE	FPW	Sw	1	DRD	DRD	BRN				[ ]							
K-A01p	Honor Medal	BGE	FPW	Sw	1	RED	RED	BRN				[ ]							
K-A01q	Honor Medal	BGE	FPW	Sw	1	LRD	LRD	MBN				[ ]							
K-A01r	Honor Medal	BGE	FPW	Sw	1	RED	RED	MBN				[ ]							
K-A01s	Honor Medal	BGE	FPW	Sw	1	DRD	DRD	LBN				[ ]							
K-A01t	Honor Medal	BGE	CPW	Sw	1	LRD	LRD	BGE				[ ]							
K-A01u	Honor Medal	BGE	CPW	CD	1	DRD	DRD	BGE				[ ]							
K-A01v	Honor Medal	BGE	CPW	CD	1	LRD	LRD	BGE				[ ]							
K-A01w	Honor Medal	BGE	CPW	CD	1	RED	RED	BGE				[ ]							
K-A01x	Honor Medal	BGE	MPW	CD	3	LRD	LRD	BGE						[ ]					
K-A01y	Honor Medal	BGE	MPW	CD	3	RED	RED	BGE								[ ]			
K-A01z	Honor Medal	BGE	MPW	CD	3	LRD	LRD	BGE						[ ]					
K-A01aa	Honor Medal	BGE	MTL	CD	3	RED	RED	BGE					[ ]						Wide Border
K-A01ab	Honor Medal	BGE	MTR	CD	3	LRD	LRD	BGE						[ ]		[ ]			
K-A01ac	Honor Medal	BGE	MTL	CD	3	LRD	LRD	BGE											[ ] MPL
K-A01ad	Honor Medal	BGE	MTL	CE	3	LRD	LRD	BGE											[ ] MPL
K-A01ae	Honor Medal	BGE	MTL	CE	3	RED	RED	BGE								[ ]			Thick Knot/Border
K-A01af	Honor Medal	BGE	MTB	CE	3	DRD	DRD	BGE								[ ]			
K-A01ag	Honor Medal	BGE	MTB	CE	3	LRD	LRD	BGE								[ ]			
K-A01ah	Honor Medal	BGE	MTB	CE	3	RED	RED	BGE											[ ] MP1
K-A01ai	Honor Medal	BGE	MTB	CE	3	DRD	DRD	BGE								[ ]			[ ] MP1 Thick Knot/Border

Nmbr	Insignia	Bkgd	Fab	Emb	Tp	Right	Left	Border	CB	GB	PB	GP	LO	LG	WP	WL	LO1	FDL	Misc
K-A02a	Heroism Award	OWT	MTL	Sw	1	RED	RED	OWT			[ ]								
K-A02b	Heroism Award	OWT	MTL	Sw	1	LRD	LRD	OWT			[ ]								[ ] IVO PB
K-A02c	Heroism Award	OWT	MTL	Sw	1	LRD	LRD	OWT					[ ]						Thin knot
K-A02d	Heroism Award	OWT	FPW	Sw	1	RED	RED	OWT						[ ]					
K-A02e	Heroism Award	OWT	MTB	Sw	1	DRD	DRD	OWT			[ ]								
K-A02f	Heroism Award	WHT	MTB	CD	1	LRD	LRD	WHT			[ ]								
K-A02g	Heroism Award	OWT	MTB	CD	1	RED	RED	OWT			[ ]								[ ] YEL PB
K-A02h	Heroism Award	OWT	MTR	CD	3	LRD	LRD	OWT				[ ]		[ ]		[ ]			
K-A02i	Heroism Award	OWT	MTR	CD	3	LRD	LRD	OWT								[ ]			Thick Knot
K-A02j	Heroism Award	OWT	MTL	CD	3	LRD	LRD	OWT								[ ]			[ ] MWP
K-A02k	Heroism Award	OWT	FPW	CE	3	LRD	LRD	OWT								[ ]			
K-A02l	Heroism Award	OWT	FPW	CE	3	LRD	LRD	OWT								[ ]			Thin Knot
K-A02m	Heroism Award	OWT	MTR	CE	3	LRD	LRD	OWT								[ ]			Thick Knot
K-A02n	Heroism Award	WHT	MTR	CD	3	CAR	CAR	WHT									[ ]		

Nmbr	Insignia	Bkgd	Fab	Emb	Tp	Right	Left	Border	CB	GB	PB	GP	LO	LG	WP	WL	LO1	FDL	Misc
K-A03a	Medal of Merit	KHA	CTL	Sw	1	BLU	GLD	BRN	[ ]										
K-A03b	Medal of Merit	LKH	FTR	Sw	1	DBL	YEL	BRN		[ ]									
K-A03c	Medal of Merit	LKH	FTR	Sw	1	BLU	YEL	BRN		[ ]									
K-A03d	Medal of Merit	LKH	FTL	Sw	1	BLU	YEL	BRN		[ ]		[ ]							
K-A03e	Medal of Merit	LKH	FTL	Sw	1	BLU	GLD	BRN		[ ]		[ ]							
K-A03f	Medal of Merit	BGE	FPW	Sw	1	BLU	YEL	MBN		[ ]		[ ]							
K-A03g	Medal of Merit	BGE	FPW	Sw	1	BLU	GLD	BRN		[ ]									

---

[40] The original K-system was in Arapaho I, 1976, by Albertus Hoogeveen and Richard H. Breithaupt, Jr. This listing may be reproduced (NOT ELECTRONICALLY) for your personal use only. A guide to all abbreviations used in these tables can be found following the applicable table.

Nmbr	Insignia	Bkgd	Fab	Emb	Tp	Right	Left	Border	CB	GB	PB	GP	LO	LG	WP	WL	LO1	FDL	Misc
K-A03h	Medal of Merit	BGE	FPW	Sw	1	BLU	YEL	LBN		[ ]		[ ]							
K-A03i	Medal of Merit	LKH	FTR	Sw	1	BLU	GLD	BRN		[ ]									Thin knot
K-A03j	Medal of Merit	BGE	CPW	Sw	1	BLU	YEL	BGE		[ ]									
K-A03k	Medal of Merit	BGE	CPW	Sw	1	MBL	LYL	BGE		[ ]		[ ]							[ ] Pelon
K-A03l	Medal of Merit	BGE	CPW	CD	1	MBL	LYL	BGE		[ ]									
K-A03m	Medal of Merit	BGE	MTB	CD	1	LBL	LYL	TAN		[ ]									
K-A03n	Medal of Merit	BGE	MTB	CD	1	BLU	PYL	TAN		[ ]									
K-A03o	Medal of Merit	BGE	MTR	CD	3	PBL	PYL	BGE						[ ]					
K-A03p	Medal of Merit	BGE	MPW	CD	3	PBL	PYL	BGE						[ ]		[ ]			
K-A03q	Medal of Merit	BGE	MTL	CD	3	PBL	PYL	BGE											[ ] MWP [ ] MW1 [ ] PLO Wide Border
K-A03r	Medal of Merit	BGE	MTL	CD	3	PBL	PYL	BGE					[ ]	[ ]	[ ]				[ ] MLG [ ] PLO [ ] MPL
K-A03s	Medal of Merit	BGE	MTL	CD	3	PBL	PYL	DBG											[ ] MW1 Wide Border
K-A03t	Medal of Merit	BGE	MPW	CD	3	BLU	BYL	BGE											[ ] PLO Wide Border
K-A03u	Medal of Merit	BGE	MTL	CD	3	PBL	PYL	BGE											[ ] PW
K-A03v	Medal of Merit	BGE	MPW	CE	3	BLU	BYL	BGE											[ ] MWP Wide Border
K-A03w	Medal of Merit	BGE	MTL	CE	3	PBL	PYL	BGE								[ ]			[ ] MW1
K-A03x	Medal of Merit	BGE	MTL	CE	3	PBL	PYL	BGE								[ ]			[ ] MP1 Wide Border

B. For Distinguished Service

Nmbr	Insignia	Bkgd	Fab	Emb	Tp	Right	Left	Border	CB	GB	PB	GP	LO	LG	WP	WL	LO1	FDL	Misc
K-B01a	Silver World	R/W	FE	Sw	0a	Stars & Stripes	NBL		[ ]										BM-MTL Thick RED DBL
K-B01b	Silver World	R/W	FE	Sw	0a	Stars & Stripes	NBL			[ ]									BM-MTR Thick RED
K-B01c	Silver World	R/W	FE	Sw	0a	Stars & Stripes	NBL		[ ]										BM-MTL Thick WHT
K-B01d	Silver World	R/W	FE	Sw	0a	Stars & Stripes	NBL			[ ]									BM-MTR Thick WHT
K-B01e	Silver World	R/W	FE	Sw	0a	Stars & Stripes	NBL		[ ]										BM-MTL Thick RED BLU
K-B01f	Silver World	R/W	FE	CD	0b	Stars & Stripes	NBL			[ ]			[ ]	[ ]	[ ]				BM-MTR Thick WHT [ ] MPB
K-B01g	Silver World	R/W	FE	CD	0b	Stars & Stripes	NBL			[ ]									BM-MPW Thick WHT
K-B01h	Silver World	R/W	FE	CD	0b	Stars & Stripes	NBL							[ ]	[ ]				BM-MTR Thick RED [ ] MWP
K-B01i	Silver World	R/W	FE	CD	0b	Stars & Stripes	NBL							[ ]					BM-MTR
K-B01j	Silver World	R/W	FE	CD	0b	Stars & Stripes	NBL												BM-MTR Thick WHT [ ] MW1 DRD
K-B01k	Silver World	R/W	FE	CD	0b	Stars & Stripes	NBL												BM-MPW Thick WHT DRD [ ] MW1

Nmbr	Insignia	Bkgd	Fab	Emb	Tp	Right	Left	Border	CB	GB	PB	GP	LO	LG	WP	WL	LO1	FDL	Misc
K-B02a	Silver Buffalo	KHA	CTL	Sw	1	RED	WHT	BRN	[ ]										
K-B02b	Silver Buffalo	LKH	FTR	Sw	1	RED	WHT	BRN		[ ]									
K-B02c	Silver Buffalo	LKH	FTR	Sw	1	LRD	WHT	BRN		[ ]									
K-B02d	Silver Buffalo	LKH	FTR	Sw	1	DRD	WHT	MBN		[ ]									
K-B02e	Silver Buffalo	LKH	FTR	Sw	1	RED	WHT	MBN		[ ]									
K-B02f	Silver Buffalo	LKH	FTR	Sw	1	LRD	WHT	MBN		[ ]									
K-B02g	Silver Buffalo	LKH	FTR	Sw	1	RED	WHT	LBN		[ ]									
K-B02h	Silver Buffalo	LKH	FTR	Sw	1	LRD	WHT	LBN		[ ]									
K-B02i	Silver Buffalo	LKH	FTL	Sw	1	DRD	WHT	MRN			[ ]								
K-B02j	Silver Buffalo	LKH	FTL	Sw	1	RED	WHT	MBN			[ ]								
K-B02k	Silver Buffalo	LKH	FTL	Sw	1	LRD	WHT	MRN			[ ]								
K-B02l	Silver Buffalo	LKH	FTL	Sw	1	RED	WHT	LBN			[ ]								
K-B02m	Silver Buffalo	LKH	FTL	Sw	1	LRD	WHT	LBN			[ ]								
K-B02n	Silver Buffalo	BGE	CPW	Sw	1	RED	WHT	DBG			[ ]								
K-B02o	Silver Buffalo	BGE	CPW	Sw	1	LRD	WHT	DBG			[ ]								
K-B02p	Silver Buffalo	BGE	MTR	CD	3	DRD	WHT	BGE						[ ]					30° Angle
K-B02q	Silver Buffalo	BGE	MTR	CD	3	RED	WHT	BGE						[ ]					30° Angle Wide Border
K-B02r	Silver Buffalo	BGE	MTR	CD	3	LRD	WHT	LBG						[ ]					30° Angle
K-B02s	Silver Buffalo	BGE	MTR	CD	3	DRD	WHT	BGE						[ ]					30° Angle Thin Knot
K-B02t	Silver Buffalo	BGE	MPW	CD	3	RED	WHT	DBG					[ ]						
K-B02u	Silver Buffalo	BGE	MTR	CD	3	LRD	WHT	BGE							[ ]				60° Angle
K-B02v	Silver Buffalo	BGE	MTL	CD	3	RED	WHT	BGE							[ ]	[ ]			[ ] MLG
K-B02w	Silver Buffalo	BGE	MPW	CD	3	LRD	WHT	BGE											[ ] MPL Thin Knot
K-B02x	Silver Buffalo	BGE	MTB	CD	3	RED	WHT	BGE											[ ] PLG
K-B02y	Silver Buffalo	BGE	MPW	CE	3	LRD	WHT	BGE											[ ] MLG
K-B02z	Silver Buffalo	BGE	MTL	CE	3	RED	WHT	BGE											[ ] MLO Thick BDR
K-B02aa	Silver Buffalo	BGE	FPW	CE	3	RED	WHT	BGE									[ ]		
K-B02ab	Silver Buffalo	BGE	MTB	CE	3	DRD	WHT	BGE									[ ]		[ ] MP1
K-B02ac	Silver Buffalo	BGE	MTB	CE	3	DRD	WHT	BGE									[ ]		Thick Border

Nmbr	Insignia	Bkgd	Fab	Emb	Tp	Right	Left	Border	CB	GB	PB	GP	LO	LG	WP	WL	LO1	FDL	Misc
K-B03a	Silver Antelope	KHA	CTL	Sw	1	ORG	WHT	BRN	[ ]										Thick Knot
K-B03b	Silver Antelope	KHA	CTL	Sw	1	DOR	WHT	BRN		[ ]									

Nmbr	Insignia	Bkgd	Fab	Emb	Tp	Right	Left	Border	CB	GB	PB	GP	LO	LG	WP	WL	LO1	FDL	Misc
K-B03c	Silver Antelope	KHA	FTR	Sw	1	DOR	WHT	MBN		[ ]									
K-B03d	Silver Antelope	KHA	FTR	Sw	1	ORG	WHT	MBN		[ ]									
K-B03e	Silver Antelope	KHA	FTR	Sw	1	POR	WHT	LBN		[ ]									
K-B03f	Silver Antelope	KHA	FTR	Sw	1	ORG	WHT	BRN				[ ]							Thin Knot
K-B03g	Silver Antelope	KHA	FTR	Sw	1	LOR	WHT	MBN				[ ]							Thick Knot
K-B03h	Silver Antelope	KHA	FTL	Sw	1	DOR	WHT	BRN				[ ]							[ ]MPB Thin Knot
K-B03i	Silver Antelope	KHA	FTL	Sw	1	ORG	WHT	MBN											[ ]MPB Thin Knot
K-B03j	Silver Antelope	LKH	FTL	Sw	1	DGD	WHT	MBN			[ ]								Thin Knot
K-B03k	Silver Antelope	LKH	CPW	Sw	1	LOR	WHT	MBN			[ ]								Thin Knot
K-B03l	Silver Antelope	LKH	FPW	Sw	1	DOR	WHT	BRN					[ ]						
K-B03m	Silver Antelope	LKH	FPW	Sw	1	DOR	WHT	BRN			[ ]								
K-B03n	Silver Antelope	LKH	FPW	Sw	1	DOR	WHT	MBR			[ ]								
K-B03o	Silver Antelope	LKH	FPW	Sw	1	DOR	WHT	LBN			[ ]								
K-B03p	Silver Antelope	LKH	FPW	Sw	1	ORG	WHT	LBN			[ ]								
K-B03q	Silver Antelope	LKH	FPW	Sw	1	ORG	WHT	LBN			[ ]								Thin Knot
K-B03r	Silver Antelope	LKH	FPW	Sw	1	LOR	WHT	BRN			[ ]								
K-B03s	Silver Antelope	LKH	FPW	Sw	1	LOR	WHT	LBN			[ ]								
K-B03t	Silver Antelope	LKH	FPW	Sw	1	GLD	WHT	BRN			[ ]								Thin Knot
K-B03u	Silver Antelope	LKH	FPW	Sw	1	DGD	WHT	BRN					[ ]						
K-B03v	Silver Antelope	DBG	CPW	Sw	1	DOR	WHT	BGE			[ ]								
K-B03w	Silver Antelope	DBG	CPW	Sw	1	ORG	WHT	BGE			[ ]								
K-B03x	Silver Antelope	DBG	MPW	Sw	1	DOR	WHT	DBG			[ ]								Thick Knot
K-B03y	Silver Antelope	BGE	FPW	Sw	1	DOR	WHT	BGE											[ ]EGS PB
K-B03z	Silver Antelope	DBG	MPW	CD	1	ORG	WHT	DBG			[ ]								
K-B03aa	Silver Antelope	DBG	MPW	CD	1	DOR	WHT	BGE			[ ]								
K-B03ab	Silver Antelope	DBG	MPW	CD	1	LOR	WHT	BGE			[ ]								
K-B03ac	Silver Antelope	DBG	MPW	CD	1	DGD	WHT	BGE			[ ]								
K-B03ad	Silver Antelope	BGE	MPW	CD	3	LOR	WHT	BGE						[ ]	[ ]				[ ]MPL
K-B03ae	Silver Antelope	BGE	MPW	CD	3	DGD	WHT	BGE											[ ]MPL
K-B03af	Silver Antelope	BGE	MPW	CD	3	DGD	WHT	BGE											[ ]MPL Thick Knot
K-B03ag	Silver Antelope	BGE	MTL	CD	3	LOR	WHT	BGE						[ ]					
K-B03ah	Silver Antelope	BGE	MTL	CD	3	DGD	WHT	BGE						[ ]					[ ]MPL
K-B03ai	Silver Antelope	DBG	MPW	CE	3	LOR	WHT	BGE							[ ]				[ ]MPL
K-B03aj	Silver Antelope	DBG	MPW	CE	3	DGD	WHT	BGE							[ ]				[ ]MLO
K-B03ak	Silver Antelope	BGE	MTR	CE	3	LOR	WHT	BGE											[ ]MLO
K-B03al	Silver Antelope	BGE	MTR	CE	3	DGD	WHT	BGE											[ ]MLO
K-B03am	Silver Antelope	BGE	MTL	CE	3	LOR	WHT	BGE											[ ]PLO
K-B03an	Silver Antelope	BGE	MTL	CE	3	LOR	WHT	BGE								[ ]			[ ]MW1 [ ]MP1
K-B03ao	Silver Antelope	BGE	MTL	CE	3	DGD	WHT	BGE								[ ]			
K-B03ap	Silver Antelope	BGE	MTL	CE	3	DGD	WHT	BGE								[ ]			[ ]MW1 Thick Knot

Nmbr	Insignia	Bkgd	Fab	Emb	Tp	Right	Left	Border	CB	GB	PB	GP	LO	LG	WP	WL	LO1	FDL	Misc
K-B04a	Silver Beaver	KHA	CTL	Sw	1	LBL	WHT	KHA	[ ]	[ ]									
K-B04b	Silver Beaver	KHA	CTL	Sw	1	BLU	WHT	KHA	[ ]										
K-B04c	Silver Beaver	KHA	CTL	Sw	1	DBL	WHT	KHA	[ ]	[ ]									
K-B04d	Silver Beaver	KHA	CTL	Sw	1	BLU	WHT	KHA	[ ]										
K-B04e	Silver Beaver	LKH	FTR	Sw	1	DBL	WHT	BRN	[ ]										
K-B04f	Silver Beaver	LKH	FTR	Sw	1	BLU	WHT	BRN	[ ]										
K-B04g	Silver Beaver	LKH	FTR	Sw	1	BLU	WHT	KHA	[ ]	[ ]									
K-B04h	Silver Beaver	LKH	FTR	Sw	1	LBL	WHT	KHA											[ ]BLU GP
K-B04i	Silver Beaver	LKH	FTL	Sw	1	DPB	WHT	BRN			[ ]								
K-B04j	Silver Beaver	LKH	FTL	Sw	1	DBL	WHT	KHA			[ ]								
K-B04k	Silver Beaver	LKH	FTL	Sw	1	BLU	WHT	KHA			[ ]								
K-B04l	Silver Beaver	LKH	FTL	Sw	1	BLU	WHT	BRN			[ ]								
K-B04m	Silver Beaver	LKH	FTL	Sw	1	BLU	WHT	KHA			[ ]								
K-B04n	Silver Beaver	LKH	FTL	Sw	1	LBL	WHT	BRN			[ ]								
K-B04o	Silver Beaver	LKH	FTL	Sw	1	LBL	WHT	KHA			[ ]								
K-B04p	Silver Beaver	LKH	FTL	Sw	1	LBL	WHT	KHA			[ ]								Thick Knot
K-B04q	Silver Beaver	NBL	FL	Sw	1	DBL	WHT	BLK	[ ]										
K-B04r	Silver Beaver	NBL	FL	Sw	1	WHT	BLU	DBL	[ ]										Reverse error
K-B04s	Silver Beaver	NBL	FL	Sw	1	OWT	LBL	DBL	[ ]										Reverse error Thick Knot
K-B04t	Silver Beaver	NBL	FL	Sw	1	BLU	WHT	NBL		[ ]									
K-B04u	Silver Beaver	NBL	FL	Sw	1	BLU	OWT	NBL		[ ]									
K-B04v	Silver Beaver	NBL	FL	Sw	1	DBL	OWT	DBL			[ ]								Thick Knot
K-B04w	Silver Beaver	NBL	FL	Sw	1	DBL	WHT	DBL			[ ]								
K-B04x	Silver Beaver	NBL	FL	Sw	1	LBL	WHT	BLU			[ ]								
K-B04y	Silver Beaver	IVO	MTL	Sw	1	DBL	WHT	IVO	[ ]										
K-B04z	Silver Beaver	OWT	MTL	Sw	1	BLU	WHT	OWT	[ ]										

Nmbr	Insignia	Bkgd	Fab	Emb	Tp	Right	Left	Border	CB	GB	PB	GP	LO	LG	WP	WL	LO1	FDL	Misc
K-B04aa	Silver Beaver	OWT	MTL	Sw	1	LBL	WHT	OWT	[ ]										
K-B04ab	Silver Beaver	WHT	MTL	Sw	1	BLU	WHT	WHT		[ ]									
K-B04ac	Silver Beaver	FGN	FTL	Sw	1	DBL	WHT	FGN	[ ]										
K-B04ad	Silver Beaver	FGN	FTL	Sw	1	BLU	WHT	FGN	[ ]										
K-B04ae	Silver Beaver	FGN	MTL	Sw	1	DBL	WHT	FGN	[ ]										
K-B04af	Silver Beaver	FGN	MTL	Sw	1	BLU	WHT	FGN	[ ]										
K-B04ag	Silver Beaver	FGN	MTR	Sw	1	BLU	WHT	FGN		[ ]									
K-B04ah	Silver Beaver	FGN	MTR	Sw	1	LBL	WHT	FGN			[ ]								
K-B04ai	Silver Beaver	BGE	FPW	Sw	1	DBL	WHT	BRN	[ ]										
K-B04aj	Silver Beaver	BGE	FPW	Sw	1	DBL	WHT	LBN	[ ]										
K-B04ak	Silver Beaver	BGE	FPW	Sw	1	BLU	WHT	BRN	[ ]										On Board
K-B04al	Silver Beaver	BGE	FPW	Sw	1	BLU	WHT	BRN	[ ]										Thick Knot
K-B04am	Silver Beaver	BGE	FPW	Sw	1	BLU	WHT	MBN		[ ]									
K-B04an	Silver Beaver	BGE	FPW	Sw	1	BLU	WHT	LBN		[ ]									
K-B04ao	Silver Beaver	BGE	FPW	Sw	1	LBL	WHT	LBN	[ ]										
K-B04ap	Silver Beaver	BGE	FPW	Sw	1	LBL	WHT	MBN		[ ]									
K-B04aq	Silver Beaver	BGE	CPW	Sw	1	DBL	WHT	BGE	[ ]										
K-B04ar	Silver Beaver	BGE	CPW	Sw	1	BLU	WHT	BGE	[ ]		[ ]								[ ] Pelon
K-B04as	Silver Beaver	DBG	MTR	Sw	1	DBL	WHT	DBG	[ ]										
K-B04at	Silver Beaver	DBG	MTR	Sw	1	BLU	WHT	DBG	[ ]										
K-B04au	Silver Beaver	BGE	MTB	Sw	1	BLU	WHT	BGE	[ ]			[ ]							
K-B04av	Silver Beaver	BGE	MTB	Sw	1	DBL	WHT	BGE				[ ]							
K-B04aw	Silver Beaver	BGE	MTB	CD	1	BLU	WHT	LBG	[ ]										
K-B04ax	Silver Beaver	BGE	MTR	CD	1	LBU	WHT	LBG				[ ]							
K-B04ay	Silver Beaver	BGE	MTL	CD	1	BLU	WHT	LBG				[ ]							
K-B04az	Silver Beaver	BGE	MTB	CD	1	DLB	WHT	LBG				[ ]							
K-B04ba	Silver Beaver	BGE	MTB	CD	1	BLU	WHT	LBG				[ ]							
K-B04bb	Silver Beaver	BGE	MTB	CD	1	LBL	WHT	TAN				[ ]							Thick Knot
K-B04bc	Silver Beaver	BGE	MTB	CE	1	DBL	WHT	BGE				[ ]							
K-B04bd	Silver Beaver	BGE	MTB	CE	1	DBL	WHT	LBG				[ ]							Thick Knot
K-B04be	Silver Beaver	BGE	MTL	CE	1	BLU	WHT	LBG				[ ]							
K-B04bf	Silver Beaver	BGE	MTB	CE	1	BLU	WHT	LBG				[ ]							[ ] LW
K-B04bg	Silver Beaver	BGE	MTL	CE	1	MBL	WHT	LTN				[ ]							
K-B04bh	Silver Beaver	BGE	MTR	CE	1	MBL	WHT	LTN				[ ]							
K-B04bi	Silver Beaver	BGE	MTR	CE	1	LBL	WHT	LTN				[ ]							Thick Knot
K-B04bj	Silver Beaver	BGE	MTL	CE	1	LBL	WHT	LTN									[ ]		Thick Border
K-B04bk	Silver Beaver	BGE	MTL	CE	1	BLU	WHT	LTN									[ ]		
K-B04bl	Silver Beaver	BGE	MTL	CE	1	MBL	WHT	LTN									[ ]		Thick Border
K-B04bm	Silver Beaver	BGE	MTR	CE	1	LBL	WHT	LTN									[ ]		[ ] 2010
K-B04bn	Silver Beaver	BGE	MTR	CE	1	MBL	WHT	LTN									[ ]		
K-B04bo	Silver Beaver	BGE	MTB	CE	1	MBL	WHT	LTN										[ ]	
K-B04bp	Silver Beaver	BGE	MTR	CE	1	BLU	WHT	LTN										[ ]	

Nmbr	Insignia	Bkgd	Fab	Emb	Tp	Overhand	Border	CB	GB	PB	GP	LO	LG	WP	WL	LO1	FDL	Misc
K-B05a	Award of Merit	MBL	MTL	Sw	10	SMY	SMY	[ ]	[ ]									60° Angle
K-B05b	Award of Merit	MBL	FTR	Sw	10	SMY	SMY				[ ]							60° Angle
K-B05c	Award of Merit	NBL	MTL	Sw	10	SMY	SMY	[ ]	[ ]									[ ] MPB 60° Angle
K-B05d	Award of Merit	NBL	MTR	Sw	10	SMY	SMY		[ ]	[ ]								45° Angle
K-B05e	Award of Merit	BLU	FPW	Sw	10	SMY	SMY	[ ]										
K-B05f	Award of Merit	BLU	FPW	Sw	10	MSV	MSV	[ ]										
K-B05g	Award of Merit	RBL	MPW	Sw	10	SMY	SMY	[ ]	[ ]									
K-B05h	Award of Merit	RBL	FTR	Sw	10	SMY	SMY	[ ]										[ ] BLU PB Thin Knot 60° Angle
K-B05i	Award of Merit	DBL	MTL	Sw	10	SMY	SMY	[ ]										45° Angle
K-B05j	Award of Merit	BLU	MTB	Sw	10	SMY	SMY	[ ]	[ ]									
K-B05k	Award of Merit	DBL	MTR	Sw	10	SMY	SMY	[ ]	[ ]									Thin Bdr/Knot 45° Angle
K-B05l	Award of Merit	DBL	MPW	Sw	10	SMY	SMY	[ ]										Thick Knot
K-B05m	Award of Merit	BLU	MTR	Sw	10	SMY	SMY	[ ]										
K-B05n	Award of Merit	RBL	MPW	Sw	10	SMY	SMY											[ ] BLU PB
K-B05o	Award of Merit	NBL	FTR	Sw	10	MSV	MSV		[ ]									Thick Border/Knot
K-B05p	Award of Merit	DBL	MPW	CD	10	MSV	MSV		[ ]									Thick Bdr/Knot
K-B05q	Award of Merit	BLU	MTL	CD	10	MSV	MSV		[ ]									60° Angle
K-B05r	Award of Merit	NBL	MPW	CD	10	MSV	MSV		[ ]									Thick Border/Knot
K-B05s	Award of Merit	DBL	MTL	CD	10	MSV	MSV		[ ]			[ ]	[ ]	[ ]				60° Angle
K-B05t	Award of Merit	DBL	MTB	Sw	10	SMY	SMY					[ ]						Thin Border/Knot
K-B05u	Award of Merit	DBL	MTB	CD	10	MSV	MSV					[ ]						Thick Knot
K-B05v	Award of Merit	DBL	MTR	CD	10	MSV	MSV					[ ]	[ ]	[ ]				60° Angle
K-B05w	Award of Merit	BLU	MTL	CD	10	MSV	MSV		[ ]						[ ]			45° Angle

Nmbr	Insignia	Bkgd	Fab	Emb	Tp	Overhand	Border	CB	GB	PB	GP	LO	LG	WP	WL	LO1	FDL	Misc
K-B05x	Award of Merit	BBL	MTB	CE	10	MCV	MSV				[ ]							Thick Border/Knot
K-B05y	Award of Merit	BLU	MTL	CE	10	MSV	MSV								[ ]			Thin Border/Knot
K-B05z	Award of Merit	DBL	MTR	CE	10	MSV	MSV						[ ]			[ ]	[ ]	45° Angle

Nmbr	Insignia	Bkgd	Fab	Emb	Tp	Right	Left	Border	CB	GB	PB	GP	LO	LG	WP	WL	LO1	FDL	Misc
K-B06a	OA Dist Service	CAR	MTL	Sw	1	OWT	OWT	CAR	[ ]										
K-B06b	OA Dist Service	DRD	MTL	Sw	1	OWT	OWT	CAR	[ ]										
K-B06c	OA Dist Service	DRD	MTL	Sw	1	OWT	OWT	RED				[ ]							
K-B06d	OA Dist Service	DRD	MTL	Sw	1	OWT	OWT	LRD		[ ]	[ ]								Thick Knot
K-B06e	OA Dist Service	RED	MTL	CD	1	WHT	WHT	RED				[ ]							Thin Knot
K-B06f	OA Dist Service	LRD	FPW	Sw	1	OWT	OWT	RED		[ ]									
K-B06g	OA Dist Service	DRD	MTB	CD	1	OWT	OWT	DRD		[ ]									
K-B06h	OA Dist Service	RED	MTB	CD	1	OWT	OWT	RED		[ ]									Thick Knot
K-B06i	OA Dist Service	RED	MTR	CD	3	OWT	OWT	LRD				[ ]							
K-B06j	OA Dist Service	LRD	MTR	CD	3	OWT	OWT	LRD				[ ]							
K-B06k	OA Dist Service	DRD	MPW	CD	3	OWT	OWT	RED						[ ]					[ ] RED LO Wide Border
K-B06l	OA Dist Service	DRD	MTR	CD	3	OWT	OWT	LRD						[ ]					[ ] GRN LO
K-B06m	OA Dist Service	DRD	MTR	CD	3	OWT	OWT	LRD								[ ]			[ ] MWL
K-B06n	OA Dist Service	DRD	MTL	CE	3	OWT	OWT	RED						[ ]					
K-B06o	OA Dist Service	DRD	MTR	CE	3	OWT	OWT	RED									[ ]		[ ] PL1 Wide Border
K-B06p	OA Dist Service	DRD	MTR	CE	3	WHT	WHT	RED										[ ]	[ ] MP1 Wide Border
K-B06q	OA Dist Service	DRD	MTR	CE	3	LGY	LGY	RED										[ ]	Wide Border

Nmbr	Insignia	Bkgd	Fab	Emb	Tp	Right	Left	Border	CB	GB	PB	GP	LO	LG	WP	WL	LO1	FDL	Misc
K-B07a	George Meany	W/R	FE	Sw	4	DBL	DBL	W/R	[ ]										BM-MTL Reverse error
K-B07b	George Meany	R/W	FE	Sw	4	DBL	DBL	R/W	[ ]										BM-MTL
K-B07c	George Meany	R/W	FE	Sw	4	DBL	DBL	R/W	[ ]										BM-FPW
K-B07d	George Meany	R/W	FE	CD	4	NBL	NBL	R/W	[ ]										BM-MTB [ ] YEL PB DRD
K-B07e	George Meany	R/W	FE	CD	4	BLU	BLU	R/W	[ ]										BM-MTB DRD
K-B07f	George Meany	R/W	FE	CE	4	BLU	BLU	R/W		[ ]	[ ]								BM-MTB

Nmbr	Insignia	Bkgd	Fab	Emb	Tp	Right	Left	Border	CB	GB	PB	GP	LO	LG	WP	WL	LO1	FDL	Misc
K-B08a	Spurgeon Award	DOL	FPW	Sw	5	GLD	GLD	GLD	[ ]										Misprint
K-B08b	Spurgeon Award	DOL	MPW	Sw	1	DGD	DGD	DGD	[ ]										
K-B08c	Spurgeon Award	BLK	MPW	Sw	1	GLD	GLD	GLD	[ ]										
K-B08d	Spurgeon Award	BLK	MPW	CD	1	LGD	LGD	LGD	[ ]										
K-B08e	Spurgeon Award	OLV	MTR	CD	3	GLD	GLD	GLD						[ ]					[ ] MLG
K-B08f	Spurgeon Award	OLV	MPW	CD	3	GLD	GLD	GLD						[ ]					
K-B08g	Spurgeon Award	OLV	MTL	CD	3	LGD	LGD	LGD						[ ]					
K-B08h	Spurgeon Award	OLV	MTR	CD	3	LGD	LGD	LGD						[ ]					
K-B08i	Spurgeon Award	OLV	MTR	CD	3	LGD	LGD	LGD											[ ] MLG
K-B08j	Spurgeon Award	OLV	MPW	CD	3	DGD	DGD	DGD											[ ] PL1 Thick Border
K-B08k	Spurgeon Award	OLV	MPW	CD	3	GLD	GLD	GLD											[ ] MW1 [ ] PL1 Thick Bdr
K-B08l	Spurgeon Award	OLV	FPW	CD	3	LGD	LGD	LGD											[ ] PL1

Nmbr	Insignia	Bkgd	Fab	Emb	Tp	Right	Left	Border	CB	GB	PB	GP	LO	LG	WP	WL	LO1	FDL	Misc
K-B09a	Whitney M Young	BGE	CPW	Sw	1	BLK	WHT	RED	[ ]	[ ]									
K-B09b	Whitney M Young	DBG	FPW	Sw	1	BLK	WHT	DRD	[ ]	[ ]									
K-B09c	Whitney M Young	BGE	CPW	CD	3	BLK	WHT	LRD		[ ]									Wide Border
K-B09d	Whitney M Young	BGE	MTB	CD	1	BLK	WHT	RED					[ ]						
K-B09e	Whitney M Young	BGE	MPW	CD	1	BLK	WHT	RED					[ ]						
K-B09f	Whitney M Young	DBG	MPW	CD	1	BLK	WHT	DRD					[ ]						
K-B09g	Whitney M Young	BGE	MTB	CD	1	BLK	WHT	DRD					[ ]						Thick Knot
K-B09h	Whitney M Young	BGE	MTB	CD	1	BLK	WHT	DRD					[ ]						Thin knot
K-B09i	Whitney M Young	BGE	MTL	CD	3	BLK	WHT	LRD											[ ] MWL [ ] PLO Thick Bdr
K-B09j	Whitney M Young	BGE	MTL	CD	1	BLK	WHT	RED					[ ]						
K-B09k	Whitney M Young	BGE	MTL	CD	3	BLK	WHT	LRD					[ ]						[ ] MWL Thick Knot/Border
K-B09l	Whitney M Young	BGE	MTR	CD	1	BLK	WHT	RED					[ ]						Thin Knot
K-B09m	Whitney M Young	BGE	MTB	CE	1	BLK	WHT	RED					[ ]						
K-B09n	Whitney M Young	BGE	MTR	CE	1	BLK	WHT	RED						[ ][41]					
K-B09o	Whitney M Young	BGE	MTL	CE	1	BLK	WHT	RED								[ ]			Thick knot
K-B09p	Whitney M Young	BGE	MTL	CE	1	BLK	WHT	RED									[ ][42]		
K-B09q	Whitney M Young	BGE	MTR	CE	1	BLK	WHT	RED									[ ]		
K-B09r	Whitney M Young	BGE	MTR	CE	1	BLK	WHT	RED									[ ]		

Nmbr	Insignia	Bkgd	Fab	Emb	Tp	Right	Left	Border	CB	GB	PB	GP	LO	LG	WP	WL	LO1	FDL	Misc
K-B10a	James E West	BGE	CPW	Sw	1	YGN	DGD	LRD	[ ]										
K-B10b	James E West	BGE	MTB	Sw	1	GRN	DGD	LRD	[ ]										
K-B10c	James E West	BGE	MTB	Sw	1	GRN	CSK	RED											[ ] Pelon

[41] Upper BLK rope offset and BLK ropes touch in center.

[42] Upper BLK rope offset and BLK ropes touch in center.

Nmbr	Insignia	Bkgd	Fab	Emb	Tp	Right	Left	Border	CB	GB	PB	GP	LO	LG	WP	WL	LO1	FDL	Misc
K-B10d	James E West	BGE	MTB	Sw	1	BGN	GLD	DRD											[ ] PW
K-B10e	James E West	BGE	MTB	Sw	1	DPN	LYL	DRD	[ ]										
K-B10f	James E West	BGE	MTB	CD	1	DPG	LGD	DRD	[ ]										Thin Knot
K-B10g	James E West	BGE	MTB	CD	1	DPG	LGD	DRD	[ ]										
K-B10h	James E West	BGE	MTB	CD	1	DGN	LYL	DRD	[ ]										
K-B10i	James E West	BGE	MTR	CD	3	GRN	GLD	LRD		[ ]									
K-B10j	James E West	BGE	MPW	CD	3	GRN	DGD	LRD		[ ]									Thick Border Cut Oversize
K-B10k	James E West	BGE	MPW	CD	3	LGN	DGD	LRD		[ ]									Thick Border Cut Oversize
K-B10l	James E West	BGE	MPW	CD	3	YGN	GLD	LRD		[ ]									Thick Border Cut Oversize
K-B10m	James E West	BGE	MTR	CD	3	GRN	DGD	LRD		[ ]									Thick Border Cut Oversize
K-B10n	James E West	BGE	MTB	CD	1	DPG	LGD	DRD			[ ]								
K-B10o	James E West	BGE	MTB	CD	1	DPG	LGD	RED			[ ]								
K-B10p	James E West	BGE	MTB	CD	1	DGN	LGD	DRD			[ ]								
K-B10q	James E West	BGE	MTB	CD	1	DGN	CSK	DRD			[ ]								
K-B10r	James E West	BGE	MTB	CD	1	GRN	YEL	DRD			[ ]								
K-B10s	James E West	BGE	MTB	CE	1	DGN	YEL	DRD			[ ]								
K-B10t	James E West	BGE	MTB	CE	1	GRN	LYL	DRD			[ ]								
K-B10u	James E West	BGE	MTB	CE	1	GRN	LGD	DRD			[ ]								
K-B10v	James E West	BGE	MTB	CE	1	BGN	LYL	DRD			[ ]								
K-B10w	James E West	BGE	MTB	CE	1	BGN	LYL	DRD			[ ]								Thick Knot
K-B10x	James E West	BGE	MTB	CE	1	BGN	LGD	RED			[ ]								
K-B10y	James E West	BGE	MTB	CE	1	YGN	LGD	RED			[ ]								
K-B10z	James E West	BGE	MTL	CE	1	DPG	GLD	RED								[ ]			Thin Knot
K-B10aa	James E West	BGE	MTR	CE	1	DGN	GLD	RED								[ ]			Thin Knot
K-B10ab	James E West	BGE	MTR	CE	1	GRN	LDG	RED								[ ]			Thin Knot/Border
K-B10ac	James E West	BGE	MTR	CE	1	GRN	LGD	RED								[ ]			

Nmbr	Insignia	Bkgd	Fab	Emb	Tp	Right	Left	Border	CB	GB	PB	GP	LO	LG	WP	WL	LO1	FDL	Misc
K-B11a	Community Org[43]	PUR	MTB	Sw	1	GLD	GLD	GLD				[ ]							
K-B11b	Community Org	PUR	MTB	CD	1	LGD	LGD	LGD				[ ]							
K-B11c	Community Org	PUR	MTB	CD	1	DGD	DGD	DGD				[ ]							
K-B11d	Community Org	PUR	MTL	CD	1	DGD	DGD	DGD				[ ]							
K-B11e	Community Org	PUR	MTR	CE	1	DGD	DGD	DGD											[ ] PL1
K-B11f	Community Org	PUR	MTL	CE	1	GLD	GLD	GLD											[ ] PL1 Thin Border

Nmbr	Insignia	Bkgd	Fab	Emb	Tp	Right	Left	Border	CB	GB	PB	GP	LO	LG	WP	WL	LO1	FDL	Misc
K-B12a	Asian	VIO	MTB	CD	1	OWT	DGN	DPL				[ ]							Reverse error
K-B12b	Asian	VIO	MTB	CD	1	DGN	WHT	PUR				[ ]							
K-B12c	Asian	VIO	MTR	CD	1	FGN	WHT	PUR				[ ]							
K-B12d	Asian	DVI	MPW	CD	3	FGN	WHT	PUR								[ ]			Thick Border
K-B12e	Asian	VIO	MTL	CE	1	WHT	DGN	PUR								[ ]			Reverse error

Nmbr	Insignia	Bkgd	Fab	Emb	Tp	Right	Left	Border	CB	GB	PB	GP	LO	LG	WP	WL	LO1	FDL	Misc
K-B13a	Vale La Pena	LRD	MTB	CD	1	LYL	LBL	LRD								[ ]			Reverse error Wide
K-B13b	Vale La Pena	LRD	MTB	CD	1	LYL	SBL	LRD								[ ]			Reverse / Color error Wide
K-B13c	Vale La Pena	RED	MTB	CD	1	YEL	PBL	DRD								[ ]			Reverse error
K-B13d	Vale La Pena	RED	MTB	CD	1	DYL	BLU	RED								[ ]			Reverse error
K-B13e	Vale La Pena	RED	MTB	CD	1	YEL	BLU	RED								[ ]			Reverse error
K-B13f	Vale La Pena	DRD	MTB	CE	1	DRD	YEL	RED									[ ]		

Nmbr	Insignia	Bkgd	Fab	Emb	Tp	Right	Left	Border	CB	GB	PB	GP	LO	LG	WP	WL	LO1	FDL	Misc
K-B14a	Venturing Ldrship	GRB	FE	CD	2	MSV	MSV	MSV					[ ]	[ ]		[ ]			BM-MTR [ ] MW1 [ ] WP1
K-B14b	Venturing Ldrship	GRB	FE	CD	2	MSV	MSV	MSV					[ ]	[ ]					BM-MPW
K-B14c	Venturing Ldrship	GRB	FE	CD	2	MSV	MSV	MSV						[ ]					BM-MTL
K-B14d	Venturing Ldrship	GRB	FE	CD	2	SIL	SIL	SIL						[ ]					BM-MTL [ ] MLW
K-B14e	Venturing Ldrship	GRB	FE	CD	2	MSV	MSV	MSV								[ ]			BM-MTR TBDR [ ] 1LW
K-B14f	Venturing Ldrship	GRB	FE	CD	2	DSV	DSV	DSV							[ ]				BM-MTR TBDR
K-B14g	Venturing Ldrship	GRB	FE	CD	2	SIL	SIL	SIL								[ ]			BM-MTR TBDR
K-B14h	Venturing Ldrship	GRB	FE	CD	2	DSV	DSV	DSV								[ ]			BM-MTR TBDR DRD
K-B14i	Venturing Ldrship	GRB	FE	CD	2	MSV	MSV	MSV											BM-MTR WBRD [ ] PLO [ ] LW [ ]MP1

Nmbr	Insignia	Bkgd	Fab	Emb	Tp	Right	Left	Border	CB	GB	PB	GP	LO	LG	WP	WL	LO1	FDL	Misc
K-B15a	Speaker Bank	BLK	MTR	CD	1	LMG	LMG	BLK						[ ]					Oversize
K-B15b	Speaker Bank	BLK	MTR	CD	1	LMG	LMG	BLK						[ ]					
K-B15c	Speaker Bank	BLK	MTR	CD	3	DMG	DMG	BLK											[ ] PLO

---

[43] There is a plastic back that appears to be a BSA knot. It was produced by the Pennsylvania Masonic Lodge in Harrisburg, PA. They produced to knot to award their members who received the Daniel Carter Beard award. When they discovered that the BSA was producing the knot, stopped issuing the knot and told their members to contact BSA for the knot. This knot is not being listed because it was not produced by the Boy Scouts of America.

Nmbr	Insignia	Bkgd	Fab	Emb	Tp	Right	Left	Border	CB	GB	PB	GP	LO	LG	WP	WL	LO1	FDL	Misc
K-B15d	Speaker Bank	BLK	MTL	CD	1	MGD	MGD	BLK										[ ]	60° Angle
K-B15e	Speaker Bank	BLK	MTL	CD	1	MGD	MGD	BLK										[ ]	45° Angle
K-B15f	Speaker Bank	BLK	MTR	CE	1	MGD	MGD	BLK										[ ]	

C. For Achievement

Nmbr	Insignia	Bkgd	Fab	Emb	Tp	Right	Left	Border	CB	GB	PB	GP	LO	LG	WP	WL	LO1	FDL	Misc
K-C01a	Eagle Scout[44]	KHA	CTL	Sw	1	RWB	RWB	MBN	[ ]	[ ]									
K-C01b	Eagle Scout	KHA	CTL	Sw	1	RWB	RWB	BRN	[ ]										
K-C01c	Eagle Scout	LKH	FTR	Sw	1	RWB	RWB	BRN	[ ]										DRD
K-C01d	Eagle Scout	LKH	FTL	Sw	1	RWB	RWB	BRN		[ ]									
K-C01e	Eagle Scout	LKH	FTL	Sw	1	RWB	RWB	BRN		[ ]									LRD
K-C01f	Eagle Scout	LKH	FTR	Sw	1	RWB	RWB	MBN	[ ]	[ ]									[ ] BLU PB
K-C01g	Eagle Scout	LKH	FTL	Sw	1	RWB	RWB	MBN		[ ]	[ ]								LRD
K-C01h	Eagle Scout	LKH	FTL	Sw	1	RWB	RWB	MBN			[ ]								DRD
K-C01i	Eagle Scout	LKH	FTR	Sw	1	RWB	RWB	LBN											[ ] BLU PB DRD
K-C01j	Eagle Scout	LKH	FTL	Sw	1	RWB	RWB	LBN		[ ]									DRD
K-C01k	Eagle Scout	NBL	FL	Sw	1	RWB	RWB	NBL	[ ]	[ ]									
K-C01l	Eagle Scout	NBL	FL	Sw	1	RWB	RWB	NBL	[ ]	[ ]									LRD LBL
K-C01m	Eagle Scout	NBL	FL	Sw	1	RWB	RWB	NBL	[ ]										DBL LRD
K-C01n	Eagle Scout	NBL	FL	Sw	1	RWB	RWB	NBL	[ ]										LRD
K-C01o	Eagle Scout	NBL	FL	Sw	1	RWB	RWB	NBL	[ ]										DRD DBL
K-C01p	Eagle Scout	IVO	FTL	Sw	1	RWB	RWB	IVO	[ ]										DRD
K-C01q	Eagle Scout	IVO	MTL	Sw	1	RWB	RWB	IVO	[ ]										DRD DBL
K-C01r	Eagle Scout	IVO	MTL	Sw	1	RWB	RWB	IVO	[ ]										DBL
K-C01s	Eagle Scout	WHT	MTL	Sw	1	RWB	RWB	WHT	[ ]										LRD LBL
K-C01t	Eagle Scout	WHT	MTL	Sw	1	RWB	RWB	WHT	[ ]	[ ]									DRD
K-C01u	Eagle Scout	FGN	MTL	Sw	1	RWB	RWB	FGN	[ ]	[ ]	[ ]								DBL DRD
K-C01v	Eagle Scout	FGN	MTL	Sw	1	RWB	RWB	FGN	[ ]										DRD
K-C01w	Eagle Scout	FGN	FTR	Sw	1	RWB	RWB	FGN	[ ]	[ ]	[ ]								
K-C01x	Eagle Scout	FGN	FTR	Sw	1	RWB	RWB	FGN		[ ]	[ ]								LRD
K-C01y	Eagle Scout	BGE	FPW	Sw	1	RWB	RWB	BRN	[ ]										DRD
K-C01z	Eagle Scout	BGE	FPW	Sw	1	RWB	RWB	MBN	[ ]										LBL Thick knot/Border
K-C01aa	Eagle Scout	BGE	FPW	Sw	1	RWB	RWB	MBN	[ ]	[ ]									DRD
K-C01ab	Eagle Scout	BGE	FPW	Sw	1	RWB	RWB	LBN	[ ]	[ ]									
K-C01ac	Eagle Scout	BGE	FPW	Sw	1	RWB	RWB	LBN	[ ]	[ ]									DRD
K-C01ad	Eagle Scout	BGE	CPW	Sw	1	RWB	RWB	DBG	[ ]										DBL DRD
K-C01ae	Eagle Scout	DBG	MTB	Sw	1	RWB	RWB	DBG	[ ]	[ ]									[ ] Pelon DRD
K-C01af	Eagle Scout	DBG	CPW	Sw	1	RWB	RWB	DBG	[ ]	[ ]									LRD
K-C01ag	Eagle Scout	DBG	MTB	Sw	1	RWB	RWB	DBG	[ ]										DBL LRD
K-C01ah	Eagle Scout	DBG	MTB	Sw	1	RWB	RWB	DBG	[ ]										Thick Knot Wide Border
K-C01ai	Eagle Scout	DBG	MTB	Sw	1	RWB	RWB	DBG	[ ]										
K-C01aj	Eagle Scout	BGE	MTB	CD	1	RWB	RWB	DTN	[ ]										DRD
K-C01ak	Eagle Scout	BGE	MTB	CD	1	RWB	RWB	LBG	[ ]			[ ]							
K-C01al	Eagle Scout	BGE	MTB	CD	1	RWB	RWB	TAN	[ ]										DRD
K-C01am	Eagle Scout	BGE	MTR	CD	1	RWB	RWB	BGE	[ ]										Thin Border
K-C01an	Eagle Scout	BGE	MTL	CD	1	RWB	RWB	BGE				[ ]							[ ] PLO DRD
K-C01ao	Eagle Scout	BGE	MTL	CD	1	RWB	RWB	BGE				[ ]							DBL DRD
K-C01ap	Eagle Scout	BGE	MTB	CD	1	RWB	RWB	LBG				[ ]							DBL
K-C01aq	Eagle Scout	DBG	MTB	CD	1	RWB	RWB	ECR				[ ]							LRD
K-C01ar	Eagle Scout	BGE	MTB	CD	1	RWB	RWB	BGE				[ ]							
K-C01as	Eagle Scout	BGE	MTR	CE	1	RWB	RWB	TAN				[ ]							30° Angle
K-C01at	Eagle Scout	DBG	MTB	CE	1	RWB	RWB	DBG				[ ]	[ ]						
K-C01au	Eagle Scout	DBG	MTB	CE	1	RWB	RWB	DBG						[ ]					DRD
K-C01av	Eagle Scout	DBG	MTB	CE	1	RWB	RWB	DBG				[ ]							Thick BDR
K-C01aw	Eagle Scout	BGE	MTL	CE	1	RWB	RWB	TAN				[ ]							
K-C01ax	Eagle Scout	BGE	MTR	CE	1	RWB	RWB	BGE				[ ]							
K-C01ay	Eagle Scout	DBG	MTL	CE	1	RWB	RWB	BGE				[ ]							LRD
K-C01az	Eagle Scout	BGE	MTL	CE	1	RWB	RWB	LBG								[ ]			Thin Knot/BDR
K-C01ba	Eagle Scout	BGE	MTL	CE	1	RWB	RWB	TAN								[ ]			Thin Knot/BDR
K-C01bb	Eagle Scout	BGE	MTR	CE	1	RWB	RWB	LBG								[ ]			
K-C01bc	Eagle Scout	BGE	MTR	CE	1	RWB	RWB	TAN								[ ]			
K-C01bd	Eagle Scout	BGE	MTB	CE	1	RWB	RWB	LBG									[ ]		
Nmbr	**Insignia**	**Bkgd**	**Fab**	**Emb**	**Tp**	**Right**	**Left**	**Border**	**CB**	**GB**	**PB**	**GP**	**LO**	**LG**	**WP**	**WL**	**LO1**	**FDL**	**Misc**
K-C02a	Quartermaster	KHA	CTL	Sw	1	DBL	DBL	BRN	[ ]										
K-C02b	Quartermaster	KHA	CTL	Sw	1	BLU	BLU	MBN	[ ]	[ ]									
K-C02c	Quartermaster	LKH	FTR	Sw	1	LBL	LBL	BRN	[ ]										

---

[44] The standard color for the Eagle Scout knot is RED and BLU, all others are listed.

Nmbr	Insignia	Bkgd	Fab	Emb	Tp	Right	Left	Border	CB	GB	PB	GP	LO	LG	WP	WL	LO1	FDL	Misc
K-C02d	Quartermaster	LKH	FTL	Sw	1	BLU	BLU	BRN			[ ]								
K-C02e	Quartermaster	NBL	FL	Sw	1	BLU	BLU	BLK	[ ]										
K-C02f	Quartermaster	NBL	FL	Sw	1	EGS	EGS	NBL	[ ]										
K-C02g	Quartermaster	NBL	FL	Sw	1	WHT	WHT	NBL	[ ]	[ ]									
K-C02h	Quartermaster	EGS	MTL	Sw	1	NBL	NBL	EGS	[ ]										
K-C02i	Quartermaster	OWT	MTL	Sw	1	DBL	DBL	EGS	[ ]	[ ]	[ ]		[ ]						
K-C02j	Quartermaster	OWT	MTL	Sw	1	NBL	NBL	EGS		[ ]	[ ]								
K-C02k	Quartermaster	OWT	MTL	Sw	1	PUR	PUR	EGS	[ ]										
K-C02l	Quartermaster	WHT	FTL	Sw	1	DBL	DBL	EGS	[ ]										
K-C02m	Quartermaster	WHT	FPW	Sw	1	PUR	PUR	OWT		[ ]									
K-C02n	Quartermaster	WHT	FPW	Sw	1	NBL	NBL	OWT		[ ]									
K-C02o	Quartermaster	WHT	MPW	CD	1	DBL	DBL	OWT	[ ]	[ ]									
K-C02p	Quartermaster	WHT	MTB	CD	1	DBL	DBL	WHT		[ ]									
K-C02q	Quartermaster	WHT	MTR	CD	3	MNB	MNB	OWT				[ ]		[ ]		[ ]		[ ]	YL
K-C02r	Quartermaster	WHT	MTR	CD	3	MNB	MNB	WHT								[ ]			
K-C02s	Quartermaster	OWT	MTL	CD	3	MNB	MNB	OWT								[ ]			
K-C02t	Quartermaster	WHT	MTL	CD	3	MNB	MNB	WHT					[ ]					[ ]	YL
K-C02u	Quartermaster	WHT	MTR	CE	3	MNB	MNB	WHT								[ ]			[ ]WP1 [ ]MW1 Wide Border
K-C02v	Quartermaster	WHT	MPW	CE	3	MNB	MNB	WHT								[ ]			Wide Border

Nmbr	Insignia	Bkgd	Fab	Emb	Tp	Right	Left	Border	CB	GB	PB	GP	LO	LG	WP	WL	LO1	FDL	Misc
K-C03	Ace Award	LBL	FTL	Sw	1	BLU	RED	BLU	[ ]										

Nmbr	Insignia	Bkgd	Fab	Emb	Tp	Right	Left	Border	CB	GB	PB	GP	LO	LG	WP	WL	LO1	FDL	Misc
K-C04	Ranger Award[45]	GRN	MTR	Sw	1	GRN	BRN	GRN	[ ]										

Nmbr	Insignia	Bkgd	Fab	Emb	Tp	Right	Left	Border	CB	GB	PB	GP	LO	LG	WP	WL	LO1	FDL	Misc
K-C05	Silver Award #1	NBL	CTL	Sw	1	RED	GLD	NBL	[ ]										

Nmbr	Insignia	Bkgd	Fab	Emb	Tp	Right	Left	Border	CB	GB	PB	GP	LO	LG	WP	WL	LO1	FDL	Misc
K-C06a	Silver Award #2	RWB	FE	Sw	2	MNG	MNG	MNG	[ ]	[ ]									BM-CTR
K-C06b	Silver Award #2	RWB	FE	Sw	2	DGY	DGY	DGY	[ ]										BM-CTR
K-C06c	Silver Award #2	RWB	FE	Sw	2	STG	STG	STG	[ ]										BM-CTR
K-C06d	Silver Award #2	RWB	FE	Sw	2	LST	LST	LST	[ ]										BM-CTR
K-C06e	Silver Award #2	RWB	FE	Sw	2	LST	LST	LST	[ ]										BM-CTR Thin Knot
K-C06f	Silver Award #2	RWB	FE	Sw	2	SGY	SGY	SGY				[ ]							BM-CTR
K-C06g	Silver Award #2	RWB	FE	Sw	2	LGY	LGY	LGY				[ ]							BM-CTR
K-C06h	Silver Award #2	RWB	FE	Sw	2	LST	LST	LST	[ ]										BM-MPW DBL
K-C06i	Silver Award #2	RWB	FE	Sw	2	SIL	SIL	SIL	[ ]										BM-CTL DBL
K-C06j	Silver Award #2	RWB	FE	Sw	2	STG	STG	STG			[ ]	[ ]							BM-CTR DBL
K-C06k	Silver Award #2	RWB	FE	Sw	2	STG	STG	STR			[ ]	[ ]							BM-MPW
K-C06l	Silver Award #2	RWB	FE	Sw	2	LST	LST	LST				[ ]							BM-MPW
K-C06m	Silver Award #2	RWB	FE	Sw	2	MGY	MGY	MGY				[ ]							BM-CTR
K-C06n	Silver Award #2	RWB	FE	Sw	2	LRG	LRG	LRG					[ ]						BM-MPW
K-C06o	Silver Award #2	RWB	FE	Sw	2	RGY	RGY	RGY					[ ]		[ ]				BM-MTB
K-C06p	Silver Award #2	RWB	FE	Sw	2	DSG	DSG	DSG						[ ]					BM-MTR Thick Bdr
K-C06q	Silver Award #2	RWB	FE	Sw	2	DSG	DSG	DSG						[ ]					BM-MTR Thick Knot/Border
K-C06r	Silver Award #2	RWB	FE	Sw	1	RGY	RGY	RGY					[ ]						BM-MPW Thin Knot DRD DBL
K-C06s	Silver Award #2	RWB	FE	Sw	1	RGY	RGY	RGY					[ ]						BM-MTB Thin Knot
K-C06t	Silver Award #2	RWB	FE	Sw	1	RGY	RGY	RGY					[ ]						BM-MTB Thin Knot SWT
K-C06u	Silver Award #2	RWB	FE	Sw	1	LRG	LRG	LRG					[ ]						BM-MTL
K-C06v	Silver Award #2	RWB	FE	Sw	1	LRG	LRG	LRG					[ ]						BM-MPW
K-C06w	Silver Award #2	RWB	FE	Sw	1	LGY	LGY	LGY					[ ]						BM-MPW
K-C06x	Silver Award #2	RWB	FE	CD	1	LRG	LRG	LRG					[ ]						BM-MTL
K-C06y	Silver Award #2	RWB	FE	CD	1	RGY	RGY	RGY					[ ]	[ ]					BM-MTB Thick Knot
K-C06z	Silver Award #2	RWB	FE	CD	1	RGY	RGY	RGY					[ ]						BM-MTB Thin Knot DRD DBL
K-C06aa	Silver Award #2	RWB	FE	CD	2	DSG	DSG	DSG						[ ]	[ ]	[ ]			BM-MTR
K-C06ab	Silver Award #2	RWB	FE	CD	2	DSG	DSG	DSG						[ ]	[ ]	[ ]			BM-MTL
K-C06ac	Silver Award #2	RWB	FE	CD	2	DSG	DSG	DSG						[ ]					BM-MPW
K-C06ad	Silver Award #2	RWB	FE	CD	2	LSG	LSG	LSG						[ ]					BM-MTR
K-C06ae	Silver Award #2	RWB	FE	CE	2	SGY	SGY	SGY								[ ]			BM-MTR
K-C06af	Silver Award #2	RWB	FE	CE	2	LSG	LSG	LSG						[ ]					BM-MTR SWT
K-C06ag	Silver Award #2	RWB	FE	CE	2	DSG	DSG	DSG								[ ]			BM-MTR SWT
K-C06ah	Silver Award #2	RWB	FE	CE	2	DSG	DSG	DSG						[ ]	[ ]				BM-MTR [ ]WP1
K-C06ai	Silver Award #2	RWB	FE	CE	2	DSG	DSG	DSG									[ ]		BM-MTR Wide Bdr
K-C06aj	Silver Award #2	RWB	FE	CE	2	SGY	SGY	SGY											BM-MPW [ ]WP1 [ ]MW1 [ ]MW1 Wide Bdr

---

[45] There have been numerous backs reported that range from tan to light yellow. All varieties have been used (washed), and we have never found any mint varieties with a background color other than GRN. National Supply had one of every knot issued over the years on display prior to moving from New Jersey. The only knot they had was the one on GRN.

Nmbr	Insignia	Bkgd	Fab	Emb	Tp	Right	Left	Border	CB	GB	PB	GP	LO	LG	WP	WL	LO1	FDL	Misc
K-C07a	Arrow of Light	KHA	FTL	Sw	1	DPN	RED	YEL	[ ]										
K-C07b	Arrow of Light	KHA	FTL	Sw	1	WLG	RED	CSK	[ ]										
K-C07c	Arrow of Light	KHA	FTL	Sw	1	DGN	RED	YEL	[ ]										
K-C07d	Arrow of Light	KHA	FTL	Sw	1	GRN	RED	CSK	[ ]										
K-C07e	Arrow of Light	KHA	FTL	Sw	1	DPG	RED	YEL	[ ]										
K-C07f	Arrow of Light	KHA	FTL	Sw	1	DGN	RED	CSK	[ ]	[ ]									
K-C07g	Arrow of Light	KHA	FTL	Sw	1	DBR	RED	YEL	[ ]	[ ]									
K-C07h	Arrow of Light	KHA	FTL	Sw	1	DPG	RED	CSK		[ ]									
K-C07i	Arrow of Light	KHA	FTL	Sw	1	GRN	DRD	CSK		[ ]									
K-C07j	Arrow of Light	BGE	FPW	Sw	1	BGN	RED	GLD	[ ]										
K-C07k	Arrow of Light	LBG	FPW	Sw	1	BGN	RED	YEL	[ ]										
K-C07l	Arrow of Light	LBG	FPW	Sw	1	DBR	DRD	YEL	[ ]										
K-C07m	Arrow of Light	BGE	FPW	Sw	1	YGN	RED	DGD	[ ]										Thick Knot/Border
K-C07n	Arrow of Light	LBG	FPW	Sw	1	DGN	DRD	CSK	[ ]										
K-C07o	Arrow of Light	BGE	FPW	Sw	1	DBR	DRD	GLD	[ ]										
K-C07p	Arrow of Light	BGE	FPW	Sw	1	BGN	LRD	LGD	[ ]										Thick Knot/Border
K-C07q	Arrow of Light	BGE	FPW	Sw	1	DBR	DRD	LGD		[ ]									
K-C07r	Arrow of Light	BGE	FPW	Sw	1	YGN	DRD	LGD		[ ]									Thick Knot
K-C07s	Arrow of Light	BGE	MPW	Sw	1	BGN	RED	YEL	[ ]										Thin Knot
K-C07t	Arrow of Light	BGE	MPW	Sw	1	DGN	LRD	YEL	[ ]										
K-C07u	Arrow of Light	BGE	MPW	Sw	1	DPG	RED	YEL	[ ]										
K-C07v	Arrow of Light	BGE	MPW	Sw	1	LBG	LRD	YEL	[ ]										
K-C07w	Arrow of Light	BGE	MPW	Sw	1	GRN	LRD	YEL		[ ]									
K-C07x	Arrow of Light	BGE	CPW	Sw	1	LRD	DGN	YEL	[ ]										Reverse Error
K-C07y	Arrow of Light	BGE	CPW	Sw	1	RED	GRN	YEL	[ ]										Reverse Error Thin Knot
K-C07z	Arrow of Light	BGE	CPW	Sw	1	LRD	GRN	YEL	[ ]										Reverse Error
K-C07aa	Arrow of Light	BGE	CPW	Sw	1	RED	DGN	YEL	[ ]										Reverse Error Thin Knot
K-C07ab	Arrow of Light	BGE	CPW	Sw	1	LRD	BGN	YEL	[ ]										Reverse Error
K-C07ac	Arrow of Light	BGE	CPW	Sw	1	LRD	DGN	LYL	[ ]										Reverse Error
K-C07ad	Arrow of Light	BGE	CPW	Sw	1	DGN	RED	LGD	[ ]										
K-C07ae	Arrow of Light	BGE	CPW	Sw	1	DGN	LRD	LGD	[ ]										
K-C07af	Arrow of Light	BGE	CPW	Sw	1	DGN	LRD	YEL	[ ]										
K-C07ag	Arrow of Light	BGE	MTR	Sw	1	DBR	DRD	GLD									[ ]		PW
K-C07ah	Arrow of Light	BGE	MTB	CD	1	BGN	MRD	LGD				[ ]							
K-C07ai	Arrow of Light	BGE	MTB	CD	1	BGN	MRD	YEL				[ ]							
K-C07aj	Arrow of Light	BGE	MTB	CD	1	BGN	RED	DGD				[ ]							Thick Knot
K-C07ak	Arrow of Light	BGE	MTB	CD	1	DBR	LRD	DGD				[ ]							
K-C07al	Arrow of Light	BGE	MTB	CD	1	DBR	MRD	DGD				[ ]							
K-C07am	Arrow of Light	BGE	MTB	CD	1	DBR	MRD	GLD				[ ]							
K-C07an	Arrow of Light	BGE	MTB	CD	1	DBR	MRD	LGD				[ ]							
K-C07ao	Arrow of Light	BGE	MTB	CD	1	DPG	RED	LGD				[ ]							
K-C07ap	Arrow of Light	BGE	MTB	CD	1	DYG	MRD	GLD				[ ]							
K-C07aq	Arrow of Light	BGE	MTB	CD	1	FGN	LRD	GLD				[ ]							
K-C07ar	Arrow of Light	BGE	MTB	CD	1	LGN	MRD	LGD				[ ]							Thick Knot
K-C07as	Arrow of Light	BGE	MTL	CD	1	DBR	MRD	DGD				[ ]							Thick Knot
K-C07at	Arrow of Light	BGE	MTB	CD	1	BGN	MRD	LGD				[ ]					[ ]		PLO
K-C07au	Arrow of Light	BGE	MTR	CD	1	BGN	MRD	LGD				[ ]							60° Angle
K-C07av	Arrow of Light	BGE	FPW	CD	1	DBR	LRD	GLD				[ ]							
K-C07aw	Arrow of Light	BGE	MTR	CD	1	BGN	MRD	GLD				[ ]							
K-C07ax	Arrow of Light	BGE	MTB	CD	1	DYG	MRD	GLD				[ ]							
K-C07ay	Arrow of Light	BGE	MTB	CD	1	DYG	MRD	GLD				[ ]							
K-C07az	Arrow of Light	BGE	MTB	CD	1	LBG	RED	GLD				[ ]							Thin Knot
K-C07ba	Arrow of Light	BGE	MTB	CD	1	GRN	LRD	LGD				[ ]							Thin Knot
K-C07bb	Arrow of Light	BGE	MTB	CE	1	LGN	LRD	LYL				[ ]							
K-C07bc	Arrow of Light	BGE	MTB	CE	1	GRN	LRD	LGD				[ ]	[ ]						
K-C07bd	Arrow of Light	BGE	MTB	CE	1	LGN	LRD	LGD					[ ]						
K-C07be	Arrow of Light	BGE	MTB	CE	1	LGN	MRD	LGD					[ ]						
K-C07bf	Arrow of Light	BGE	MTB	CE	1	GRN	MRD	DGD					[ ]						
K-C07bg	Arrow of Light	BGE	FPW	CE	1	BGN	RED	LGD					[ ]						
K-C07bh	Arrow of Light	BGE	MPW	CE	1	LGN	LRD	LGD					[ ]						
K-C07bi	Arrow of Light	BGE	MPW	CE	1	GRN	MRD	LGD					[ ]						
K-C07bj	Arrow of Light	BGE	MTL	CE	1	DBR	LRD	YEL				[ ]							
K-C07bk	Arrow of Light	BGE	MTL	CE	1	DBR	LRD	LGD				[ ]							
K-C07bl	Arrow of Light	BGE	MTL	CE	1	DBR	MRD	YEL				[ ]							60° Angle
K-C07bm	Arrow of Light	BGE	MTL	CE	1	DBR	MRD	LYL				[ ]							Thick Knot
K-C07bn	Arrow of Light	BGE	MTB	CE	1	DBR	RED	LYL				[ ]							Thick Knot
K-C07bo	Arrow of Light	BGE	MTB	CE	1	DBR	RED	LGD								[ ]			

Nmbr	Insignia	Bkgd	Fab	Emb	Tp	Right	Left	Border	CB	GB	PB	GP	LO	LG	WP	WL	LO1	FDL	Misc
K-C07bp	Arrow of Light	BGE	MTB	CE	1	DBR	RED	LYL								[ ]			30° Angle Thin Border
K-C07bq	Arrow of Light	BGE	MTL	CE	1	DGN	MRD	LYL								[ ]			Thin Knot/Border
K-C07br	Arrow of Light	BGE	MTL	CE	1	DBR	MRD	LYL									[ ]		60° Angle
K-C07bs	Arrow of Light	BGE	MTB	CE	1	BGN	RED	LGD									[ ]		30° Angle Thin Border
K-C08	Hornaday Award	BGE	CPW	Sw	1	WBG	WBG	BGE			[ ]								
K-C09a	Silver Award #3	G/W	FE	Sw	2	GRY	GRY	SMY			[ ]								BM-MPW DGN
K-C09b	Silver Award #3	G/W	FE	CD	2	LGY	LGY	MSV			[ ]								BM-MPW DGN
K-C09c	Silver Award #3	G/W	FE	CD	2	GRY	GRY	DMS			[ ]								BM-MPW DGN
K-C09d	Silver Award #3	G/W	FE	CD	3	LGY	LGY	MSV			[ ]								BM-MPW
K-C09e	Silver Award #3	G/W	FE	CD	3	LGY	LGY	MSV						[ ]		[ ]			BM-MTR
K-C09f	Silver Award #3	G/W	FE	CE	3	LGY	LGY	MSV								[ ]			BM-MTR
K-C09g	Silver Award #3	G/W	FE	CE	3	LGY	LGY	MSV					[ ]			[ ]			BM-MPW
K-C09h	Silver Award #3	G/W	FE	CE	3	LGY	LGY	MSV											BM-MPW [ ] MW1 Wide Bdr
K-C09i	Silver Award #3	G/W	FE	CE	3	LGY	LGY	MSV											BM-MTR [ ] MW1 Wide Bdr
K-C10a	NESA Life Mbr	BGE	MTL	CE	1	RWB	RWB	MSV						[ ]					Oversize
K-C10b	NESA Life Mbr	BGE	MTL	CD	1	RWB	RWB	MSV						[ ]		[ ]			DRD
K-C10c	NESA Life Mbr	BGE	MTL	CE	1	RWB	RWB	DMS						[ ]					Thin Border LBL
K-C10d	NESA Life Mbr	BGE	MTR	CE	1	RWB	RWB	DMS						[ ]					Thin Border
K-C10e	NESA Life Mbr	BGE	MTL	CE	1	RWB	RWB	DMS						[ ]		[ ]			Thick Border
K-C10f	NESA Life Mbr	BGE	MTL	CE	1	RWB	RWB	DMS								[ ]			

D. For the Church

Nmbr	Insignia	Bkgd	Fab	Emb	Tp	Right	Left	Border	CB	GB	PB	GP	LO	LG	WP	WL	LO1	FDL	Misc
K-D01a	Youth Religious	DPL	FTR	Sw	1	SMY	SMY	PUR	[ ]										
K-D01b	Youth Religious	DPL	FTR	Sw	1	SMY	SMY	DPL	[ ]	[ ]	[ ]								
K-D01c	Youth Religious	PUR	MTL	Sw	1	SMY	SMY	PUR	[ ]	[ ]									BLU PB
K-D01d	Youth Religious	DLV	CPW	Sw	1	SMY	SMY	PUR	[ ]	[ ]									
K-D01e	Youth Religious	PUR	FE	Sw	1	SMY	SMY	PUR	[ ]				[ ]	[ ]					BM-MPW
K-D01f	Youth Religious	PUR	FE	Sw	1	SMY	SMY	PUR	[ ]	[ ]									BM-MTL
K-D01g	Youth Religious	PUR	FE	Sw	1	SMY	SMY	PUR	[ ]	[ ]	[ ]		[ ]	[ ]					BM-MTB [ ] Pelon
K-D01h	Youth Religious	LPR	FE	Sw	1	SMY	SMY	LPR				[ ]							BM-MTL
K-D01i	Youth Religious	PUR	FE	Sw	1	SMY	SMY	PUR						[ ]					BM-MTR
K-D01j	Youth Religious	DPL	FE	CD	1	MSV	MSV	DPL	[ ]										BM-MPW
K-D01k	Youth Religious	PUR	FE	CD	1	MSV	MSV	PUR					[ ]	[ ]					BM-MPW [ ] PLO
K-D01l	Youth Religious	PUR	FE	CD	1	MSV	MSV	PUR						[ ]					BM-MTL 30° Angle
K-D01m	Youth Religious	DPL	FE	CD	1	MSV	MSV	PUR						[ ]					BM-MTR
K-D01n	Youth Religious	DPL	FE	CD	1	MSV	MSV	DPL						[ ]	[ ]				BM-MTB Thick Bdr/Knot
K-D01o	Youth Religious	PUR	FE	CD	1	MSV	MSV	PUR						[ ]		[ ]		[ ]	BM-MTL 60° Angle
K-D01p	Youth Religious	LPR	FE	CD	1	MSV	MSV	LPR						[ ]					BM-MTB
K-D01q	Youth Religious	PUR	FE	CD	1	MSV	MSV	PUR								[ ]			BM-MTR 30° Angle
K-D02a	Adult Religious	DGY	MTL	Sw	1	PUR	PUR	SMY	[ ]										[ ] BLU PB Thick Knot
K-D02b	Adult Religious	GRY	MTR	Sw	1	PUR	PUR	SMY		[ ]									Thick Knot
K-D02c	Adult Religious	GRY	MTR	Sw	1	DPL	DPL	SMY			[ ]								Thick Knot
K-D02d	Adult Religious	DGY	MTL	Sw	1	MPR	MPR	SMY	[ ]										Thick Knot
K-D02e	Adult Religious	GRY	MTL	Sw	1	LPR	LPR	SMY	[ ]	[ ]									Thick Knot
K-D02f	Adult Religious	GRY	MTR	Sw	1	BVI	BVI	SMY	[ ]										Thick Knot
K-D02g	Adult Religious	GRY	MTR	Sw	1	BVI	BVI	SMY		[ ]									
K-D02h	Adult Religious	DGY	MPW	Sw	1	DPL	DPL	SMY	[ ]										
K-D02i	Adult Religious	GRY	MTR	Sw	1	DLV	DLV	SMY		[ ]									
K-D02j	Adult Religious	DGY	MTR	Sw	1	MPR	MPR	SMY	[ ]	[ ]									
K-D02k	Adult Religious	GRY	MTR	Sw	1	DLV	DLV	SMY	[ ]										Thin Knot
K-D02l	Adult Religious	GRY	MPW	Sw	1	MLV	MLV	SMY				[ ]							Thin Knot
K-D02m	Adult Religious	GRY	MTR	Sw	1	MPL	MPL	SMY	[ ]										Thin Knot
K-D02n	Adult Religious	GRY	MTR	Sw	1	LBV	LBV	SMY	[ ]										Thin Knot
K-D02o	Adult Religious	GRY	MTB	Sw	1	BVI	BVI	SMY	[ ]										
K-D02p	Adult Religious	GRY	MTB	Sw	1	DBV	DBV	SMY	[ ]										Thin Knot
K-D02q	Adult Religious	GRY	MTB	CD	1	DBV	DBV	SMY	[ ]										Thick Border
K-D02r	Adult Religious	GRY	MPW	CD	1	LAV	LAV	MSV	[ ]										
K-D02s	Adult Religious	GRY	MTB	CD	1	MPR	MPR	MSV	[ ]										
K-D02t	Adult Religious	GRY	MTB	CD	1	BVI	BVI	MSV	[ ]				[ ]						
K-D02u	Adult Religious	GRY	MTB	CD	1	LBV	LBV	DMS					[ ]						
K-D02v	Adult Religious	GRY	MTB	CD	1	LBV	LBV	DMS					[ ]						Thin Knot
K-D02w	Adult Religious	GRY	MTB	CD	1	BVI	BVI	SMY					[ ]						
K-D02x	Adult Religious	GRY	MTB	CD	1	BVI	BVI	DMS					[ ]						Thin Knot

Nmbr	Insignia	Bkgd	Fab	Emb	Tp	Right	Left	Border	CB	GB	PB	GP	LO	LG	WP	WL	LO1	FDL	Misc
K-D02y	Adult Religious	GRY	MTB	CD	1	BVI	BVI	SMY				[ ]							Thin Knot/Border
K-D02z	Adult Religious	GRY	MTB	CD	1	MLV	MLV	SMY				[ ]							
K-D02aa	Adult Religious	GRY	MTL	CD	1	LPR	LPR	SMY				[ ]							Thin Knot/Thick Border
K-D02ab	Adult Religious	GRY	MTL	CD	1	DLV	DLV	DMS				[ ]							Thin Border
K-D02ac	Adult Religious	DGY	MTL	CE	1	BVI	BVI	DMS				[ ]							
K-D02ad	Adult Religious	GRY	MTB	CE	1	DBL	DBL	DMS				[ ]							Thin Knot
K-D02ae	Adult Religious	DGY	MTL	CE	1	MPR	MPR	DMS				[ ]				[ ]			Thin Border
K-D02af	Adult Religious	DGY	MTR	CE	1	DLV	DLV	DMS				[ ]				[ ]			Thin Border
K-D02ag	Adult Religious	DGY	MTL	CE	1	DLV	DLV	DMS								[ ]			Thin Knot
K-D02ah	Adult Religious	DGY	MTL	CE	1	BVI	BVI	DMS								[ ]			
K-D02ai	Adult Religious	DGY	MTL	CE	1	BVI	BVI	DMS										[ ]	Thin Knot/Border

E. For Leadership

Nmbr	Insignia	Bkgd	Fab	Emb	Tp	Right	Left	Border	CB	GB	PB	GP	LO	LG	WP	WL	LO1	FDL	Misc
K-E01a	Scouter's Key	KHA	CTL	Sw	1	FGN	WHT	BRN	[ ]										
K-E01b	Scouter's Key	KHA	CTL	Sw	1	DPG	WHT	BRN	[ ]										
K-E01c	Scouter's Key	KHA	CTL	Sw	1	DGN	WHT	BRN	[ ]	[ ]									
K-E01d	Scouter's Key	LKH	FTL	Sw	1	GRN	WHT	BRN		[ ]								[ ]	MPB
K-E01e	Scouter's Key	LKH	FTL	Sw	1	GRN	WHT	MBN			[ ]								
K-E01f	Scouter's Key	LKH	FTL	Sw	1	DPG	WHT	MBN			[ ]	[ ]							
K-E01g	Scouter's Key	LKH	FTL	Sw	1	LGN	WHT	MBN				[ ]							
K-E01h	Scouter's Key	LKH	FTR	Sw	1	DGN	WHT	MBN		[ ]									Thick Knot
K-E01i	Scouter's Key	LKH	FTR	Sw	1	GRN	WHT	BRN		[ ]									Thick Knot
K-E01j	Scouter's Key	LKH	FTR	Sw	1	GRN	WHT	MBN										[ ]	BLU BP Thick Knot
K-E01k	Scouter's Key	LKH	FTR	Sw	1	LGN	OWT	LBN		[ ]									Thick Knot
K-E01l	Scouter's Key	LKH	FTR	Sw	1	LGN	OWT	MBN		[ ]									Thick Knot
K-E01m	Scouter's Key	LKH	FTR	Sw	1	LGN	WHT	LBN		[ ]									Thick Knot
K-E01n	Scouter's Key	NBL	FL	Sw	1	DPG	WHT	NBL	[ ]	[ ]									
K-E01o	Scouter's Key	NBL	FL	Sw	1	DGN	WHT	NBL	[ ]			[ ]							
K-E01p	Scouter's Key	OWT	FTL	Sw	1	DGN	WHT	OWT	[ ]										
K-E01q	Scouter's Key	WHT	FTL	Sw	1	DGN	WHT	WHT	[ ]										
K-E01r	Scouter's Key	WHT	MTL	Sw	1	DGN	WHT	WHT		[ ]									
K-E01s	Scouter's Key	FGN	MTL	Sw	1	DGN	WHT	FGN	[ ]										
K-E01t	Scouter's Key	FGN	MTL	Sw	1	GRN	WHT	FGN	[ ]	[ ]									
K-E01u	Scouter's Key	FGN	FTR	Sw	1	DGN	WHT	FGN		[ ]									
K-E01v	Scouter's Key	FGN	FTR	Sw	1	GRN	WHT	FGN				[ ]							
K-E01w	Scouter's Key	BGE	FPW	Sw	1	DGR	WHT	MBN		[ ]									
K-E01x	Scouter's Key	BGE	FPW	Sw	1	DGR	WHT	MBN				[ ]							Thick Knot
K-E01y	Scouter's Key	BGE	FPW	Sw	1	GRN	WHT	MBN				[ ]							
K-E01z	Scouter's Key	BGE	FPW	Sw	1	LGR	WHT	MBN				[ ]							
K-E01aa	Scouter's Key	BGE	FPW	Sw	1	GRN	WHT	MBN		[ ]									
K-E01ab	Scouter's Key	BGE	FPW	Sw	1	GRN	WHT	MBN				[ ]							Thin Knot
K-E01ac	Scouter's Key	BGE	FPW	Sw	1	LGR	WHT	LBN				[ ]							Thin Knot
K-E01ad	Scouter's Key	BGE	CPW	Sw	1	DGN	WHT	DBG				[ ]							
K-E01ae	Scouter's Key	BGE	CPW	Sw	1	DGN	WHT	BGE		[ ]									Thin Knot
K-E01af	Scouter's Key	BGE	CPW	Sw	1	DGN	WHT	BGE		[ ]									
K-E01ag	Scouter's Key	BGE	MTB	Sw	1	GRN	WHT	BGE						[ ]					Thin Knot
K-E01ah	Scouter's Key	BGE	MPW	Sw	1	YGN	WHT	BGE		[ ]								[ ]	Pelon
K-E01ai	Scouter's Key	BGE	MTB	Sw	1	GRN	WHT	BGE		[ ]									
K-E01aj	Scouter's Key	BGE	MTB	Sw	1	DGN	WHT	BGE		[ ]			[ ]						
K-E01ak	Scouter's Key	BGE	MTB	CD	1	LGN	WHT	TAN		[ ]									
K-E01al	Scouter's Key	BGE	MTB	CD	1	DGN	WHT	TAN						[ ]					
K-E01am	Scouter's Key	BGE	MTB	CD	1	GRN	WHT	LBG						[ ]					
K-E01an	Scouter's Key	BGE	MTB	CD	1	KGN	WHT	LBG						[ ]					
K-E01ao	Scouter's Key	BGE	MTB	CE	1	YGN	WHT	LBG						[ ]				[ ]	LW
K-E01ap	Scouter's Key	BGE	MTL	CE	1	KGN	WHT	BGE						[ ]					
K-E01aq	Scouter's Key	BGE	MTR	CE	1	YGR	WHT	LTN						[ ]		[ ]			Thick Knot
K-E01ar	Scouter's Key	BGE	MTL	CE	1	GRN	WHT	LTN								[ ]			Thick Knot

Nmbr	Insignia	Bkgd	Fab	Emb	Tp	Right	Left	Border	CB	GB	PB	GP	LO	LG	WP	WL	LO1	FDL	Misc
K-E02a	Scouter's Training	KHA	CTL	Sw	1	FGN	FGN	BRN	[ ]										
K-E02b	Scouter's Training	KHA	CTL	Sw	1	DPG	DPG	MBN	[ ]										
K-E02c	Scouter's Training	KHA	CTL	Sw	1	DEG	DEG	MBN	[ ]										
K-E02d	Scouter's Training	KHA	CTL	Sw	1	DGN	DGN	BRN	[ ]										
K-E02e	Scouter's Training	KHA	CTL	Sw	1	GRN	GRN	BRN	[ ]										
K-E02f	Scouter's Training	KHA	CTL	Sw	1	KGN	KGN	MBN	[ ]										
K-E02g	Scouter's Training	KHA	CTL	Sw	1	LGN	LGN	KHA	[ ]										
K-E02h	Scouter's Training	KHA	CTL	Sw	1	KGN	KGN	MBN	[ ]										Thin Knot
K-E02i	Scouter's Training	KHA	FTR	Sw	1	DPG	DPG	BRN		[ ]								[ ]	BLU PB

Nmbr	Insignia	Bkgd	Fab	Emb	Tp	Right	Left	Border	CB	GB	PB	GP	LO	LG	WP	WL	LO1	FDL	Misc
K-E02j	Scouter's Training	KHA	FTR	Sw	1	DGN	DGN	BRN	[ ]			[ ]							
K-E02k	Scouter's Training	KHA	FTR	Sw	1	KGN	KGN	BRN	[ ]	[ ]									
K-E02l	Scouter's Training	KHA	FTR	Sw	1	GRN	GRN	BRN	[ ]										
K-E02m	Scouter's Training	KHA	FTR	Sw	1	LGN	LGN	BRN	[ ]			[ ]							
K-E02n	Scouter's Training	KHA	FTR	Sw	1	LGN	LGN	BRN		[ ]									Thick Knot
K-E02o	Scouter's Training	KHA	FTR	Sw	1	YGN	YGN	BRN	[ ]										
K-E02p	Scouter's Training	KHA	FTL	Sw	1	DPG	DPG	BRN		[ ]									
K-E02q	Scouter's Training	LKH	FTL	Sw	1	DGN	DGN	MBN		[ ]									
K-E02r	Scouter's Training	KHA	FTL	Sw	1	GRN	GRN	MBN		[ ]									
K-E02s	Scouter's Training	KHA	FTL	Sw	1	KGN	KGN	BRN		[ ]									[ ] MPB
K-E02t	Scouter's Training	KHA	FTL	Sw	1	LGN	LGN	BRN		[ ]									
K-E02u	Scouter's Training	KHA	FTL	Sw	1	LKG	LKG	BRN		[ ]	[ ]								
K-E02v	Scouter's Training	LKH	FTL	Sw	1	YGN	YGN	BRN		[ ]									
K-E02w	Scouter's Training	DBL	MTL	Sw	1	GRN	GRN	DBL	[ ]										[ ] BLU PB
K-E02x	Scouter's Training	DBL	MTL	Sw	1	LGN	LGN	DBL	[ ]										[ ] BLU PB
K-E02y	Scouter's Training	DBL	FTL	Sw	1	DGN	DGN	DBL	[ ]										
K-E02z	Scouter's Training	DBL	FTL	Sw	1	GRN	GRN	DBL	[ ]										
K-E02aa	Scouter's Training	DBL	MTR	Sw	1	DGN	DGN	DBL		[ ]									
K-E02ab	Scouter's Training	DBL	MTR	Sw	1	GRN	GRN	DBL		[ ]									
K-E02ac	Scouter's Training	DBL	MTR	Sw	1	GRN	GRN	DBL		[ ]									Thick Knot
K-E02ad	Scouter's Training	DBL	MTR	Sw	1	LGN	LGN	PUR		[ ]									
K-E02ae	Scouter's Training	WHT	MTL	Sw	1	DPG	DPG	WHT	[ ]										
K-E02af	Scouter's Training	OWT	MTL	Sw	1	DGN	DGN	WHT	[ ]										
K-E02ag	Scouter's Training	OWT	MTL	Sw	1	DGN	DGN	OWT	[ ]										
K-E02ah	Scouter's Training	IVO	MTL	Sw	1	DGN	DGN	OWT	[ ]										
K-E02ai	Scouter's Training	IVO	MTL	Sw	1	GRN	GRN	OWT	[ ]										
K-E02aj	Scouter's Training	WHT	MTL	Sw	1	LGN	LGN	WHT				[ ]							
K-E02ak	Scouter's Training	WHT	MTL	Sw	1	LGN	LGN	OWT				[ ]							
K-E02al	Scouter's Training	FGN	MTL	Sw	1	DPG	DPG	FGN	[ ]										
K-E02am	Scouter's Training	FGN	MTL	Sw	1	DGN	DGN	FGN		[ ]									
K-E02an	Scouter's Training	FGN	MTL	Sw	1	GRN	GRN	FGN	[ ]										
K-E02ao	Scouter's Training	FGN	MTL	Sw	1	LGN	LGN	FGN	[ ]										
K-E02ap	Scouter's Training	FGN	MTR	Sw	1	BGN	BGN	FGN		[ ]									
K-E02aq	Scouter's Training	BGE	FPW	Sw	1	DPG	DPG	BRN		[ ]									
K-E02ar	Scouter's Training	BGE	FPW	Sw	1	DGN	DGN	BRN		[ ]									
K-E02as	Scouter's Training	BGE	FPW	Sw	1	KGN	KGN	BRN		[ ]									
K-E02at	Scouter's Training	BGE	FPW	Sw	1	GRN	GRN	BRN		[ ]									
K-E02au	Scouter's Training	BGE	FPW	Sw	1	GRN	GRN	BRN				[ ]							Thick Knot
K-E02av	Scouter's Training	BGE	FPW	Sw	1	LGN	LGN	BRN				[ ]							Thick Knot
K-E02aw	Scouter's Training	BGE	FPW	Sw	1	LGN	LGN	BRN		[ ]									
K-E02ax	Scouter's Training	BGE	FPW	Sw	1	YGN	YGN	BRN		[ ]									Thin Knot
K-E02ay	Scouter's Training	BGE	CPW	Sw	1	DPG	DPG	DBG		[ ]									Thick Knot
K-E02az	Scouter's Training	BGE	CPW	Sw	1	DGN	DGN	DBG		[ ]									
K-E02ba	Scouter's Training	BGE	CPW	Sw	1	GRN	GRN	BGE		[ ]									
K-E02bb	Scouter's Training	BGE	MPW	Sw	1	DPG	DPG	BGE		[ ]									
K-E02bc	Scouter's Training	BGE	MPW	Sw	1	DGN	DGN	BGE		[ ]									
K-E02bd	Scouter's Training	BGE	MTB	Sw	1	DGN	DGN	BGE				[ ]							
K-E02be	Scouter's Training	LBG	MTB	Sw	1	DGN	DGN	BGE				[ ]	[ ]						
K-E02bf	Scouter's Training	LBG	MTB	Sw	1	GRN	GRN	BGE					[ ]	[ ]					
K-E02bg	Scouter's Training	BGE	MTR	CD	1	BGN	BGN	LBG		[ ]									Thick Knot
K-E02bh	Scouter's Training	LBG	MTB	CD	1	DGN	DGN	TAN		[ ]		[ ]							
K-E02bi	Scouter's Training	BGE	MTB	CD	1	WLG	WLG	LBG				[ ]							
K-E02bj	Scouter's Training	BGE	MTB	CD	1	WLG	WLG	LBG				[ ]							Thin Knot
K-E02bk	Scouter's Training	BGE	MTB	CD	1	DGN	DGN	LBG				[ ]							
K-E02bl	Scouter's Training	BGE	MTB	CD	1	BGN	BGN	LBG				[ ]							
K-E02bm	Scouter's Training	LBG	MTB	CD	1	BGN	BGN	LBG				[ ]							
K-E02bn	Scouter's Training	BGE	MTB	CD	1	LGN	LGN	LBG				[ ]							
K-E02bo	Scouter's Training	BGE	MTB	CD	1	YGN	YGN	LBG				[ ]							
K-E02bp	Scouter's Training	BGE	MTB	CD	1	BGN	BGN	LBG				[ ]							Thin Knot
K-E02bq	Scouter's Training	BGE	MTB	CD	1	BGN	BGN	LBG				[ ]							
K-E02br	Scouter's Training	BGE	MTB	CE	1	DGN	DGN	LBG				[ ]							
K-E02bs	Scouter's Training	LBG	MTB	CD	1	DGN	DGN	LBG				[ ]							Thin Knot
K-E02bt	Scouter's Training	BGE	MTL	CE	1	GRN	GRN	LBG				[ ]							60° Angle
K-E02bu	Scouter's Training	BGE	MTL	CE	1	WLG	WLG	LBG				[ ]							60° Angle
K-E02bv	Scouter's Training	DBG	MTR	CE	1	DPG	DPG	LTN				[ ]						[ ]	Thin Border 45° Angle
K-E02bw	Scouter's Training	BGE	MTL	CE	1	WLG	WLG	TAN										[ ]	Thin Border 60° Angle
K-E02bx	Scouter's Training	LBG	MTR	CE	1	DGN	DGN	LTN										[ ]	Thin Border 45° Angle

Nmbr	Insignia	Bkgd	Fab	Emb	Tp	Right	Left	Border	CB	GB	PB	GP	LO	LG	WP	WL	LO1	FDL	Misc
K-E03	Skipper's Key	KHA	CTL	Sw	1	NBL	WHT	BRN	[ ]										
Nmbr	**Insignia**	**Bkgd**	**Fab**	**Emb**	**Tp**	**Right**	**Left**	**Border**	**CB**	**GB**	**PB**	**GP**	**LO**	**LG**	**WP**	**WL**	**LO1**	**FDL**	**Misc**
K-E04a	Den Leader Training	DBL	MTL	Sw	1	YEL	YEL	BLU	[ ]	[ ]									
K-E04b	Den Leader Training	DBL	MTR	Sw	1	YEL	YEL	DBL	[ ]										
K-E04c	Den Leader Training	DBL	MTL	Sw	1	LYL	LYL	BLU	[ ]										Thick Knot
K-E04d	Den Leader Training	DBL	MTL	Sw	1	DYL	DYL	BLU	[ ]										
K-E04e	Den Leader Training	DBL	MTL	Sw	1	DYL	DYL	BLU	[ ]										Thick Knot
Nmbr	**Insignia**	**Bkgd**	**Fab**	**Emb**	**Tp**	**Right**	**Left**	**Border**	**CB**	**GB**	**PB**	**GP**	**LO**	**LG**	**WP**	**WL**	**LO1**	**FDL**	**Misc**
K-E05a	Den Leader Coach	DBL	MTL	Sw	1	BLU	GLD	DBL	[ ]	[ ]									
K-E05b	Den Leader Coach	DBL	FTR	Sw	1	BLU	YEL	PUR	[ ]										
K-E05c	Den Leader Coach	DBL	MTL	Sw	1	LBL	YEL	DBL	[ ]										
K-E05d	Den Leader Coach	DBL	MTL	Sw	1	LBL	GLD	DBL	[ ]	[ ]									
K-E05e	Den Leader Coach	DBL	MTL	Sw	1	LBL	YEL	PUR	[ ]										
Nmbr	**Insignia**	**Bkgd**	**Fab**	**Emb**	**Tp**	**Right**	**Left**	**Border**	**CB**	**GB**	**PB**	**GP**	**LO**	**LG**	**WP**	**WL**	**LO1**	**FDL**	**Misc**
K-E06a	Pro Training Award	OWT	FE	Sw	2	BLK	BLK	BLK				[ ]							BM-MTL (WHT) Thin Knot
K-E06b	Pro Training Award	OWT	FE	Sw	2	BLK	BLK	BLK				[ ]	[ ]						BM-MTR Thin Knot
K-E06c	Pro Training Award	OWT	FE	Sw	2	BLK	BLK	BLK				[ ]							BM-FPW Thin Knot
K-E06d	Pro Training Award	OWT	FE	Sw	2	BLK	BLK	BLK											BM-MTR [ ] GRY PB Thick Knot
K-E06e	Pro Training Award	OWT	FE	Sw	2	BLK	BLK	BLK											BM-MTB [ ] DGY PB Thick Knot
K-E06f	Pro Training Award	OWT	FE	Sw	2	BLK	BLK	BLK				[ ]							BM-MTR Thick Knot
K-E06g	Pro Training Award	OWT	FE	CD	2	BLK	BLK	BLK				[ ]							BM-FPW
K-E06h	Pro Training Award	OWT	FE	CD	2	BLK	BLK	BLK				[ ]		[ ]					BM-MTR
K-E06i	Pro Training Award	OWT	FE	CE	2	BLK	BLK	BLK										[ ]	BM-MTL
Nmbr	**Insignia**	**Bkgd**	**Fab**	**Emb**	**Tp**	**Right**	**Left**	**Border**	**CB**	**GB**	**PB**	**GP**	**LO**	**LG**	**WP**	**WL**	**LO1**	**FDL**	**Misc**
K-E07a	Cubmaster Award	YEL	FPW	Sw	1	DBL	DBL	YEL	[ ]	[ ]									Thick Knot
K-E07b	Cubmaster Award	YEL	FPW	Sw	1	PBL	PBL	YEL		[ ]									Thick Knot
K-E07c	Cubmaster Award	YEL	MPW	Sw	1	BLU	BLU	DAF											[ ] Pelon
K-E07d	Cubmaster Award	YEL	FPW	Sw	1	BLU	BLU	YEL	[ ]	[ ]									
K-E07e	Cubmaster Award	YEL	FPW	Sw	1	BLU	BLU	YEL							[ ]				Thin Knot
K-E07f	Cubmaster Award	YEL	FPW	CD	1	BLU	BLU	DAF	[ ]										Thick Knot
K-E07g	Cubmaster Award	YEL	MTB	CD	1	LBL	LBL	BYL	[ ]										
K-E07h	Cubmaster Award	YEL	FPW	CD	1	DBL	DBL	DAF	[ ]										Thick Knot
K-E07i	Cubmaster Award	YEL	MTB	CD	1	PBL	PBL	YEL	[ ]	[ ]	[ ]								
K-E07j	Cubmaster Award	YEL	MTB	CD	1	LBL	LBL	YEL	[ ]	[ ]	[ ]	[ ]	[ ]						[ ] PLO
K-E07k	Cubmaster Award	YEL	MTW	CD	1	PBL	PBL	DAF				[ ]							Thick Knot
K-E07l	Cubmaster Award	YEL	MTB	CE	1	DBL	DBL	DAF				[ ]							
K-E07m	Cubmaster Award	YEL	MTB	CE	1	LBL	LBL	YEL				[ ]							[ ] LW
K-E07n	Cubmaster Award	YEL	MTB	CE	1	LBL	LBL	YEL											[ ] LW [ ] YL Thin Knot
K-E07o	Cubmaster Award	YEL	MTB	CE	1	LBL	LBL	YEL				[ ]							Thin Knot
K-E07p	Cubmaster Award	YEL	MTL	CE	1	PBL	PBL	GLD				[ ]							
K-E07q	Cubmaster Award	YEL	MTR	CE	1	LBL	LBL	YEL				[ ]							
K-E07r	Cubmaster Award	YEL	MTR	CE	1	PBL	PBL	GLD									[ ]		Thin Knot
K-E07s	Cubmaster Award	YEL	MTL	CE	1	LBL	LBL	GLD									[ ]		[ ] LG1 Thin Knot
Nmbr	**Insignia**	**Bkgd**	**Fab**	**Emb**	**Tp**	**Right**	**Left**	**Border**	**CB**	**GB**	**PB**	**GP**	**LO**	**LG**	**WP**	**WL**	**LO1**	**FDL**	**Misc**
K-E08a	Den Leader Coach	DBL	MTL	Sw	1	PBL	PBL	LPR				[ ]							
K-E08b	Den Leader Coach	DBL	MTL	Sw	1	BLU	BLU	PUR				[ ]							
K-E08c	Den Leader Coach	DBL	MPW	Sw	1	LBL	LBL	DPL				[ ]							
K-E08d	Den Leader Coach	DBL	MPW	Sw	1	LBL	LBL	PUR				[ ]							
K-E08e	Den Leader Coach	DBL	MPW	Sw	1	LBL	LBL	LPR				[ ]	[ ]						
K-E08f	Den Leader Coach	DBL	MPW	Sw	1	BLU	BLU	DBL					[ ]						
K-E08g	Den Leader Coach	DBL	MPW	CD	1	BLU	BLU	PUR				[ ]							
K-E08h	Den Leader Coach	DBL	MPW	CD	1	LBL	LBL	BLU				[ ]	[ ]						
K-E08i	Den Leader Coach	DBL	MPW	CD	1	PBL	PBL	DBL				[ ]							
K-E08j	Den Leader Coach	DBL	MPW	CD	1	PBL	PBL	BLU				[ ]							
K-E08k	Den Leader Coach	DBL	MPW	CD	1	PBL	PBL	RBL				[ ]							
K-E08l	Den Leader Coach	DBL	MPW	CD	1	DBL	DBL	PUR				[ ]	[ ]						
K-E08m	Den Leader Coach	DBL	MPW	CD	1	BLU	BLU	RBL					[ ]						
K-E08n	Den Leader Coach	DBL	MTB	CD	1	LBL	LBL	DBL				[ ]							
Nmbr	**Insignia**	**Bkgd**	**Fab**	**Emb**	**Tp**	**Right**	**Left**	**Border**	**CB**	**GB**	**PB**	**GP**	**LO**	**LG**	**WP**	**WL**	**LO1**	**FDL**	**Misc**
K-E09a	Webelos Den Ldr	YEL	MPW	Sw	1	DGD	DGD	LYL				[ ]							
K-E09b	Webelos Den Ldr	YEL	MPW	Sw	1	DGD	DGD	SFL				[ ]							Thin Knot
K-E09c	Webelos Den Ldr	YEL	MPW	Sw	1	LGD	LGD	PLY				[ ]							Thin Knot
K-E09d	Webelos Den Ldr	LYL	MPW	Sw	1	LGD	LGD	PYL				[ ]							
K-E09e	Webelos Den Ldr	YEL	MPW	Sw	1	LYL	LYL	BYL				[ ]							
K-E09f	Webelos Den Ldr	LYL	MPW	Sw	1	GLD	GLD	BYL				[ ]							

Nmbr	Insignia	Bkgd	Fab	Emb	Tp	Right	Left	Border	CB	GB	PB	GP	LO	LG	WP	WL	LO1	FDL	Misc
K-E09g	Webelos Den Ldr	YEL	MPW	CD	1	CSK	CSK	DAF	[ ]										
K-E09h	Webelos Den Ldr	LYL	MPW	Sw	1	CSK	CSK	CAN											[ ] Pelon
K-E09i	Webelos Den Ldr	LYL	MPW	Sw	1	BYL	BYL	CAN	[ ]										
K-E09j	Webelos Den Ldr	YEL	MPW	Sw	1	SGD	SGD	CAN											[ ] Pelon
K-E09k	Webelos Den Ldr	LYL	MTB	Sw	1	DYL	DYL	MYL	[ ]										
K-E09l	Webelos Den Ldr	YEL	MPW	Sw	1	GLD	GLD	PYL		[ ]									
K-E09m	Webelos Den Ldr	YEL	MPW	Sw	1	DGD	DGD	LGD		[ ]									Thick Knot
K-E09n	Webelos Den Ldr	YEL	MPW	Sw	1	DGD	DGD	PYL		[ ]									
K-E09o	Webelos Den Ldr	YEL	MPW	Sw	1	CSK	CSK	LYL		[ ]									
K-E09p	Webelos Den Ldr	YEL	MPW	Sw	1	LGD	LGD	PYL		[ ]									
K-E09q	Webelos Den Ldr	LYL	MPW	Sw	1	YEL	YEL	MYL		[ ]									
K-E09r	Webelos Den Ldr	YEL	MTB	CD	1	GLD	GLD	DAF				[ ]							
K-E09s	Webelos Den Ldr	YEL	MPW	CD	1	GLD	GLD	DAF				[ ]							
K-E09t	Webelos Den Ldr	LYL	MPW	CD	1	DGD	DGD	MYL				[ ]							
K-E09u	Webelos Den Ldr	LYL	MTB	CD	1	CSK	CSK	MYL				[ ]							Thick Knot
K-E09v	Webelos Den Ldr	LYL	MTB	CD	1	YEL	YEL	SFL				[ ]							
K-E09w	Webelos Den Ldr	LYL	MTB	CD	1	DGD	DGD	DAF				[ ]							[ ] LW
K-E09x	Webelos Den Ldr	YEL	MTB	CD	1	LYL	LYL	DAF											[ ] LW Thick Knot
K-E09y	Webelos Den Ldr	LYL	MTB	CD	1	YEL	YEL	MYL											[ ] PLO
K-E09z	Webelos Den Ldr	YEL	MTB	CD	1	YEL	YEL	SFL											[ ] PLO
K-E09aa	Webelos Den Ldr	LYL	MTB	CD	1	GLD	GLD	CAN				[ ]							
K-E09ab	Webelos Den Ldr	LYL	MTB	CD	1	GLD	GLD	CAN				[ ]							Thick Knot/Border
K-E09ac	Webelos Den Ldr	LYL	MTB	CD	1	GLD	GLD	MYL				[ ]							
K-E09ad	Webelos Den Ldr	LYL	MTB	CD	1	LYL	LYL	DAF				[ ]							Thick Knot
K-E09ae	Webelos Den Ldr	LYL	MTB	CD	1	LYL	LYL	DAF											[ ] LW
K-E09af	Webelos Den Ldr	YEL	MTB	CD	1	CSK	CSK	DAF				[ ]							
K-E09ag	Webelos Den Ldr	YEL	MTB	CE	1	DGD	DGD	DAF				[ ]							Thin Border
K-E09ah	Webelos Den Ldr	LYL	MTB	CD	1	DGD	DGD	BYL				[ ]							
K-E09ai	Webelos Den Ldr	LYL	MTR	CE	1	CSK	CSK	MYL				[ ]							
K-E09aj	Webelos Den Ldr	LYL	MTB	CE	1	CSK	CSK	MYL				[ ]							
K-E09ak	Webelos Den Ldr	LYL	MTR	CE	1	DGD	DGD	MYL				[ ]							
K-E09al	Webelos Den Ldr	LYL	MTB	CE	1	GLD	GLD	SFL											[ ] PLO
K-E09am	Webelos Den Ldr	LYL	MTB	CE	1	GLD	GLD	MYL				[ ]							[ ] LW
K-E09an	Webelos Den Ldr	LYL	MTB	CE	1	GLD	GLD	BYL				[ ]							Thick Knot
K-E09ao	Webelos Den Ldr	LYL	MTL	CE	1	CSK	CSK	YEL				[ ]							Thin Border
K-E09ap	Webelos Den Ldr	LYL	MTB	CE	1	DGD	DGD	BYL				[ ]							
K-E09aq	Webelos Den Ldr	LYL	MTB	CE	1	DGD	DGD	MYL											[ ] LW
K-E09ar	Webelos Den Ldr	LYL	MTR	CE	1	CSK	CSK	YEL								[ ]			
K-E09as	Webelos Den Ldr	LYL	MTR	CE	1	CSK	CSK	YEL								[ ]			
K-E09at	Webelos Den Ldr	LYL	MTL	CE	1	CSK	CSK	BYL								[ ]			Thin Border
K-E09au	Webelos Den Ldr	LYL	MTL	CE	1	DGD	DGD	YEL								[ ]			
K-E09av	Webelos Den Ldr	LYL	MTL	CE	1	CSK	CSK	YEL								[ ]			

Nmbr	Insignia	Bkgd	Fab	Emb	Tp	Right	Left	Border	CB	GB	PB	GP	LO	LG	WP	WL	LO1	FDL	Misc
K-E10a	Den Leader Award	DBL	MTB	Sw	1	DGD	DGD	DBL	[ ]	[ ]	[ ]								
K-E10b	Den Leader Award	DBL	FPW	Sw	1	GLD	GLD	DBL	[ ]										Thick Knot
K-E10c	Den Leader Award	DBL	MTB	Sw	1	LGD	LGD	BLU											[ ] LBL PB Thick Knot
K-E10d	Den Leader Award	DBL	MTB	Sw	1	GLD	GLD	DBL											[ ] Pelon
K-E10e	Den Leader Award	DBL	MTB	CD	1	LGD	LGD	DBL				[ ]							
K-E10f	Den Leader Award	DBL	MTB	CD	1	LGD	LGD	BLU				[ ]							
K-E10g	Den Leader Award	DBL	FPW	CD	1	GLD	GLD	DBL				[ ]		[ ]					
K-E10h	Den Leader Award	DBL	MTB	CD	1	DGD	DGD	DBL						[ ]					
K-E10i	Den Leader Award	DBL	MTR	CD	1	LGD	LGD	BLU						[ ]					
K-E10j	Den Leader Award	DBL	MTB	CD	1	GLD	GLD	DBL						[ ]					
K-E10k	Den Leader Award	DBL	MTB	CD	1	DGD	DGD	DBL						[ ]					
K-E10l	Den Leader Award	DBL	CPW	CD	1	LGD	LGD	DBL						[ ]					
K-E10m	Den Leader Award	DBL	MTB	CD	1	GLD	GLD	BLU						[ ]					Thick Knot
K-E10n	Den Leader Award	DBL	MPW	CE	1	GLD	GLD	BLU						[ ]					
K-E10o	Den Leader Award	DBL	MTR	CE	1	DGD	DGD	BLU						[ ]					
K-E10p	Den Leader Award	DBL	CPW	CE	1	GLD	GLD	BLU						[ ]					
K-E10q	Den Leader Award	DBL	MTR	CE	1	GLD	GLD	BLU						[ ]					60° Angle
K-E10r	Den Leader Award	DBL	MTL	CE	1	LGD	LGD	DBL								[ ]			
K-E10s	Den Leader Award	DBL	MPW	CE	1	LGD	LGD	DBL								[ ]			30° Angle
K-E10t	Den Leader Award	DBL	MTR	CE	1	DAF	DAF	BLU								[ ]			30° Angle

Nmbr	Insignia	Bkgd	Fab	Emb	Tp	Right	Left	Border	CB	GB	PB	GP	LO	LG	WP	WL	LO1	FDL	Misc
K-E11a	Cub Scouter Award	DBL	MTB	Sw	1	LBL	YEL	RBL	[ ]										
K-E11b	Cub Scouter Award	DBL	MTB	Sw	1	BLU	GLD	BLU		[ ]									[ ] Pelon
K-E11c	Cub Scouter Award	DBL	FPW	Sw	1	DBL	GLD	DBL											[ ] PBL PB

Nmbr	Insignia	Bkgd	Fab	Emb	Tp	Right	Left	Border	CB	GB	PB	GP	LO	LG	WP	WL	LO1	FDL	Misc
K-E11d	Cub Scouter Award	DBL	MPW	Sw	1	LBL	YEL	DBL	[ ]										
K-E11e	Cub Scouter Award	DBL	MTB	CD	1	BLU	DAF	BLU	[ ]										
K-E11f	Cub Scouter Award	DBL	MTB	CD	1	BLU	GLD	DBL	[ ]										
K-E11g	Cub Scouter Award	DBL	MTB	CD	1	LBL	GLD	BLU	[ ]										
K-E11h	Cub Scouter Award	DBL	MTB	CD	1	LBL	LGD	BLU			[ ]								
K-E11i	Cub Scouter Award	DBL	FPW	Sw	1	BLU	YEL	BLU				[ ]							
K-E11j	Cub Scouter Award	DBL	MTB	Sw	1	BLU	DYL	BLU				[ ]							
K-E11k	Cub Scouter Award	DBL	MTB	CD	1	BLU	LGD	BLU				[ ]							
K-E11l	Cub Scouter Award	DBL	MTB	CD	1	LBL	DAF	BLU				[ ]							
K-E11m	Cub Scouter Award	DBL	MTB	CD	1	LBL	YEL	BLU				[ ]							
K-E11n	Cub Scouter Award	DBL	MTB	CD	1	BLU	DAF	BLU				[ ]							
K-E11o	Cub Scouter Award	DBL	MTB	CD	1	LBL	GLD	BLU				[ ]							
K-E11p	Cub Scouter Award	DBL	MTB	CD	1	LBL	GLD	BLU				[ ]							Thick Knot/Border
K-E11q	Cub Scouter Award	DBL	MTB	CD	1	BLU	GLD	BLU				[ ]							
K-E11r	Cub Scouter Award	BLU	MTL	CE	1	PBL	GLD	BLU				[ ]							60° Angle
K-E11s	Cub Scouter Award	DBL	MTR	CE	1	PBL	LGD	DBL				[ ]				[ ]			30° Angle
K-E11t	Cub Scouter Award	DBL	CTL	CE	1	LBL	GLD	BLU				[ ]							Thin Knot
K-E11u	Cub Scouter Award	DBL	MTR	CE	1	PBL	LGD	DBL								[ ]			Thick Knot 30° Angle
K-E11v	Cub Scouter Award	DBL	MTR	CE	1	LBL	LGD	DBL								[ ]			Thin Knot 60° Angle
K-E11w	Cub Scouter Award	DBL	MTL	CE	1	PBL	GLD	BLU								[ ]			Thin Knot 60° Angle

Nmbr	Insignia	Bkgd	Fab	Emb	Tp	Right	Left	Border	CB	GB	PB	GP	LO	LG	WP	WL	LO1	FDL	Misc
K-E12a	SM Award of Merit	LTN	FPW	Sw	1	WHT	WHT	TAN	[ ]										Thick Knot
K-E12b	SM Award of Merit	LTN	FPW	Sw	1	WHT	WHT	TAN	[ ]	[ ]									
K-E12c	SM Award of Merit	DBG	CPW	Sw	1	OWT	OWT	DBG	[ ]	[ ]								[ ]	Pelon Thin Knot
K-E12d	SM Award of Merit	DBG	CPW	Sw	1	OWT	OWT	BGE	[ ]										Thick Knot
K-E12e	SM Award of Merit	DBG	CPW	Sw	1	OWT	OWT	DBG	[ ]										
K-E12f	SM Award of Merit	BGE	CPW	Sw	1	WHT	WHT	BGE	[ ]										Thin Knot
K-E12g	SM Award of Merit	BGE	MTB	CD	1	OWT	OWT	LBG	[ ]										Thin Knot
K-E12h	SM Award of Merit	BGE	CPW	Sw	1	WHT	WHT	DBG				[ ]							
K-E12i	SM Award of Merit	BGE	MTB	Sw	1	WHT	WHT	BGE				[ ]							
K-E12j	SM Award of Merit	BGE	MTB	Sw	1	WHT	WHT	LBG				[ ]							Thick Knot
K-E12k	SM Award of Merit	BGE	MPW	CD	1	WHT	WHT	LBG				[ ]							
K-E12l	SM Award of Merit	BGE	MPW	CD	1	OWT	OWT	BGE				[ ]							Thin Knot
K-E12m	SM Award of Merit	BGE	MTB	CD	1	WHT	WHT	LBG										[ ]	LW Thick Knot
K-E12n	SM Award of Merit	BGE	MTR	CD	1	OWT	OWT	LBG				[ ]							
K-E12o	SM Award of Merit	BGE	MTR	CD	1	WHT	WHT	BGE				[ ]							Thick Knot
K-E12p	SM Award of Merit	BGE	MTL	CD	1	WHT	WHT	BGE				[ ]							Thick Knot
K-E12q	SM Award of Merit	BGE	MTL	CD	1	WHT	WHT	TAN				[ ]							Thin Border
K-E12r	SM Award of Merit	BGE	MTB	CD	1	OWT	OWT	LBG				[ ]							
K-E12s	SM Award of Merit	BGE	MTB	CD	1	OWT	OWT	BGE				[ ]							

Nmbr	Insignia	Bkgd	Fab	Emb	Tp	Right	Left	Border	CB	GB	PB	GP	LO	LG	WP	WL	LO1	FDL	Misc
K-E13a	Dist Commissioner	RED	MPW	Sw	1	GRY	GRY	GRY										[ ]	RED PB
K-E13b	Dist Commissioner	RED	MTB	Sw	1	DGY	DGY	DGY	[ ]										
K-E13c	Dist Commissioner	LRD	MPW	Sw	1	MGY	MGY	MGY										[ ]	DRD PB
K-E13d	Dist Commissioner	RED	MPW	Sw	1	MGY	MGY	MGY										[ ]	DRD PB
K-E13e	Dist Commissioner	RED	MTB	Sw	1	DGY	DGY	DGY										[ ]	RED PB
K-E13f	Dist Commissioner	PRD	MTL	Sw	1	STG	STG	STG										[ ]	DRD PB
K-E13g	Dist Commissioner	RED	MTL	Sw	1	LGY	LGY	LGY	[ ]										
K-E13h	Dist Commissioner	RED	MTB	Sw	1	DGY	DGY	DGY	[ ]										
K-E13i	Dist Commissioner	RED	MTB	CD	1	SGY	SGY	SGY	[ ]			[ ]							
K-E13j	Dist Commissioner	RED	MTB	CD	1	SGY	SGY	SGY				[ ]							Wide Knot/Border
K-E13k	Dist Commissioner	RED	MTB	CD	1	SIL	SIL	SIL				[ ]							
K-E13l	Dist Commissioner	RED	MTL	CE	1	SGY	SGY	SGY				[ ]							
K-E13m	Dist Commissioner	RED	MTL	CE	1	LGY	LGY	LGY							[ ]				
K-E13n	Dist Commissioner	LRD	MTR	CE	1	LGY	LGY	LGY							[ ]				
K-E13o	Dist Commissioner	LRD	MTR	CE	1	LGY	LGY	LGY							[ ]				Thick Knot
K-E13p	Dist Commissioner	RED	MTL	CE	1	LSG	LSG	LSG							[ ]				Thin Knot/Border

Nmbr	Insignia	Bkgd	Fab	Emb	Tp	Trident Right	Trident Left	Border	CB	GB	PB	GP	LO	LG	WP	WL	LO1	FDL	Misc
K-E14a	Seabadge	GRY	MTR	Sw	11	NBL	NBL						[ ]						
K-E14b	Seabadge	GRY	FPW	Sw	11	NBL	NBL						[ ]				[ ]		PLG
K-E14c	Seabadge	GRY	MTB	Sw	11	PUR	PUR						[ ]						
K-E14d	Seabadge	LGY	FPW	CD	12	BLU	BLU					[ ]							
K-E14e	Seabadge	LGY	FPW	Sw	12	BLU	BLU					[ ]	[ ]						
K-E14f	Seabadge	DGY	MTR	Sw	13	MBL	MBL						[ ]						
K-E14g	Seabadge	DGY	MTL	Sw	13	MBL	MBL								[ ]				
K-E14h	Seabadge	DGY	MTR	Sw	14	MBL	MBL						[ ]						
K-E14i	Seabadge	DGY	MTR	Sw	11	BLU	BLU				[ ]	[ ]							

Nmbr	Insignia	Bkgd	Fab	Emb	Tp	Trident	Border	CB	GB	PB	GP	LO	LG	WP	WL	LO1	FDL	Misc
K-E14j	Seabadge	DGY	MPW	Sw	11	NBL	NBL						[ ]					
K-E14k	Seabadge	DGY	MTL	Sw	11	BLU	BLU								[ ]			
K-E14l	Seabadge	DGY	MPW	Sw	11	MBL	MBL											[ ] PLO Thin Knot
K-E14m	Seabadge	DGY	MPW	Sw	13	MBL	MBL						[ ]					
K-E14n	Seabadge	DGY	MPW	Sw	11	MBL	MBL						[ ]					
K-E14o	Seabadge	DGY	MPW	Sw	14	MBL	MBL						[ ]					
K-E14p	Seabadge	DGY	MTR	Sw	13	BLK	BLK											[ ] MLO
K-E14q	Seabadge	DGY	MTL	Sw	11	MBL	MBL								[ ]			[ ] MWL
K-E14r	Seabadge	DGY	MTR	CE	11	MBL	MBL									[ ]		
K-E14s	Seabadge	DGY	MTR	CE	13	MBL	MBL									[ ]		[ ] PL1

Nmbr	Insignia	Bkgd	Fab	Emb	Tp	Right	Left	Border	CB	GB	PB	GP	LO	LG	WP	WL	LO1	FDL	Misc
K-E15a	Tiger Cub Organizer	YEL	MTB	Sw	2	ORG	BLK	DOR	[ ]										
K-E15b	Tiger Cub Organizer	YEL	MPW	Sw	2	LOR	BLK	LOR	[ ]										
K-E15c	Tiger Cub Organizer	YEL	MPW	Sw	2	LOR	BLK	ORG		[ ]									
K-E15d	Tiger Cub Organizer	YEL	MTB	Sw	2	DOR	BLK	DOR	[ ]										
K-E15e	Tiger Cub Organizer	YEL	MTB	Sw	1	ORG	BLK	ORG	[ ]										
K-E15f	Tiger Cub Organizer	LYL	MTB	Sw	2	DOR	BLK	DOR	[ ]										Thin Knot
K-E15g	Tiger Cub Organizer	YEL	MPW	CD	2	LOR	BLK	DOR	[ ]										
K-E15h	Tiger Cub Organizer	GLD	MPW	CD	2	LOR	BLK	LOR	[ ]										
K-E15i	Tiger Cub Organizer	LYL	MTB	CD	2	PNK	BLK	PNK	[ ]										
K-E15j	Tiger Cub Organizer	LYL	MTB	CD	2	ORG	BLK	ORG											[ ] PW Thin Knot
K-E15k	Tiger Cub Organizer	LYL	MTB	CD	2	DOR	BLK	DOR											[ ] PW
K-E15l	Tiger Cub Organizer	YEL	MTB	CD	2	ORG	BLK	ORG		[ ]			[ ]						
K-E15m	Tiger Cub Organizer	YEL	MTB	CD	2	LOR	BLK	LOR		[ ]			[ ]	[ ]					
K-E15n	Tiger Cub Organizer	YEL	MTB	CD	2	DOR	BLK	DOR						[ ]					Thick Border
K-E15o	Tiger Cub Organizer	LYL	MTB	CD	2	DOR	BLK	DOR							[ ]				Thick Border
K-E15p	Tiger Cub Organizer	YEL	MTB	CD	2	DOR	BLK	DOR						[ ]					Thin Knot
K-E15q	Tiger Cub Organizer	YEL	MTB	CD	2	ORG	BLK	ORG						[ ]					Thin Knot
K-E15r	Tiger Cub Organizer	YEL	MTB	CD	2	DOR	BLK	DOR						[ ]					
K-E15s	Tiger Cub Organizer	YEL	MTB	CD	2	BOR	BLK	BOR						[ ]					
K-E15t	Tiger Cub Organizer	LYL	MTB	CD	2	LOR	BLK	ORG											[ ] LW
K-E15u	Tiger Cub Organizer	LYL	MTB	CD	2	ORG	BLK	DOR											[ ] LY
K-E15v	Tiger Cub Organizer	LYL	MTB	CD	2	ORG	BLK	DOR											[ ] LW Thin Border
K-E15w	Tiger Cub Organizer	LYL	MTB	CD	2	BOR	BLK	BOR											[ ] LW
K-E15x	Tiger Cub Organizer	LYL	MTR	CD	2	LOR	BLK	LOR						[ ]					
K-E15y	Tiger Cub Organizer	LYL	MTB	CD	2	ORG	BLK	ORG											[ ] LW [ ] LY
K-E15z	Tiger Cub Organizer	LYL	MTR	CD	2	DOR	BLK	DOR						[ ]					
K-E15aa	Tiger Cub Organizer	YEL	MTR	CD	2	PNK	BLK	PNK						[ ]					
K-E15ab	Tiger Cub Organizer	YEL	CTL	CD	2	PNK	BLK	PNK						[ ]					Thick Border
K-E15ac	Tiger Cub Organizer	LYL	MTB	CE	2	ORG	BLK	ORG											[ ] LW
K-E15ad	Tiger Cub Organizer	YEL	MTB	CE	2	BOR	BLK	BOR						[ ]					
K-E15ae	Tiger Cub Organizer	YEL	MTB	CE	2	DOR	BLK	DOR						[ ]					
K-E15af	Tiger Cub Organizer	LYL	MTR	CE	2	DOR	BLK	DOR						[ ]					
K-E15ag	Tiger Cub Organizer	LYL	CTR	CE	2	PNK	BLK	PNK						[ ]		[ ]			
K-E15ah	Tiger Cub Organizer	LYL	CTL	CE	2	PNK	BLK	PNK								[ ]			
K-E15ai	Tiger Cub Organizer	LYL	CTR	CE	2	PNK	BLK	PNK								[ ]			Thin Knot
K-E15aj	Tiger Cub Organizer	LYL	CTL	CE	2	PNK	BLK	PNK								[ ]			Thin Knot

Nmbr	Insignia	Bkgd	Fab	Emb	Tp	Right	Left	Border	CB	GB	PB	GP	LO	LG	WP	WL	LO1	FDL	Misc
K-E16a	Intnl Scouter's Awd	TAN	MTB	CD	3	PUR	WHT	LPR								[ ]			Thick Knot
K-E16b	Intnl Scouter's Awd	TAN	MTR	CD	3	PUR	WHT	PUR								[ ]			Thick Knot
K-E16c	Intnl Scouter's Awd	TAN	MTL	CE	3	PUR	WHT	PUR									[ ]		Thick Knot
K-E16d	Intnl Scouter's Awd	TAN	MPW	CE	3	LPR	WHT	LPR									[ ]		Thick Knot
K-E16e	Intnl Scouter's Awd	TAN	MPW	CE	3	LPR	WHT	LPR									[ ]		Thick Knot
K-E16f	Intnl Scouter's Awd	TAN	MTL	CE	1	DPL	WHT	DPL						[ ]					Thin Border 30° Angle
K-E16g	Intnl Scouter's Awd	TAN	MTL	CE	1	DPL	WHT	DPL											[ ] LW1 60° Angle
K-E16g	Intnl Scouter's Awd	LTN	MTL	CE	3	WHT	DPL	DPL										[ ]	Reverse Error 30° Angle

Nmbr	Insignia	Bkgd	Fab	Emb	Tp	Right	Left	Border	CB	GB	PB	GP	LO	LG	WP	WL	LO1	FDL	Misc
K-E17a	William D. Boyce	GGR	FE	CD	6	GRY	GRY	DBG								[ ]			BM-MTR DRD
K-E17b	William D. Boyce	GGR	FE	CD	6	SIL	SIL	ECR								[ ]			BM-MPW
K-E17c	William D. Boyce	GGR	FE	CD	6	GRY	GRY	BGE								[ ]			BM-MTL DRD
K-E17d	William D. Boyce	GGR	FE	CD	2	GRY	GRY	BGE							[ ]				BM-CTL [ ] MPL Wide Border
K-E17e	William D. Boyce	GGR	FE	CD	2	DGY	DGY	BGE								[ ]			BM-CTL [ ] MPL Wide Border
K-E17f	William D. Boyce	GGR	FE	CD	2	DGY	DGY	BGE									[ ]		BM-MTL
K-E17g	William D. Boyce	GGR	FE	CD	2	DGY	DGY	BGE									[ ]		BM-MTL DRD
K-E17h	William D. Boyce	GGR	FE	CD	2	GRY	GRY	BGE											BM-MTL [ ] PL1
K-E17i	William D. Boyce	GGR	FE	CE	2	GRY	GRY	BGE											BM-MPW [ ] WP1
K-E17j	William D. Boyce	GGR	FE	CE	2	DGY	DGY	BGE											BM-MTL [ ] PL1 Wide Border

Nmbr	Insignia	Bkgd	Fab	Emb	Tp	Right	Left	Border	CB	GB	PB	GP	LO	LG	WP	WL	LO1	FDL	Misc
K-E17k	William D. Boyce	GGR	FE	CE	2	DGY	DGY	BGE											BM-MPW [ ] MP1 Wide BDR
K-E17l	William D. Boyce	GGR	FE	CE	2	DGY	DGY	BGE											BM-MTL [ ] WP1 [ ] PL1 Thick BDR
K-E17m	William D. Boyce	GGR	FE	CE	2	DGY	DGY	DBG											BM-MTL [ ] MP1 DRD
Nmbr	Insignia	Bkgd	Fab	Emb	Tp	Right	Left	Border	CB	GB	PB	GP	LO	LG	WP	WL	LO1	FDL	Misc
K-E18a	Pack Trainer	YEL	MTL	CD	7	B/Y	B/Y	DBL											[ ] PLO Error
K-E18b	Pack Trainer	YEL	MTR	CD	7	B/Y	B/Y	BLU											[ ] PLO Error LRD
K-E18c	Pack Trainer	YEL	MTL	CD	1	B/Y	B/Y	DBL											[ ] LW
K-E18d	Pack Trainer	YEL	MTR	CD	1	B/Y	B/Y	BLU											[ ] LW [ ] LW1 DBL
K-E18e	Pack Trainer	YEL	MTR	CD	1	B/Y	B/Y	BLU											[ ] LW DBL Wide Border
K-E18f	Pack Trainer	YEL	MTR	CD	1	B/Y	B/Y	PBL											[ ] LW Wide Border
K-E18g	Pack Trainer	YEL	MTR	CE	1	B/Y	B/Y	BLU								[ ]			[ ] LW
K-E18h	Pack Trainer	YEL	MPW	CE	1	B/Y	B/Y	DBL											[ ] LW
K-E18i	Pack Trainer	LYL	MPW	CE	1	B/Y	B/Y	BLU											[ ] LW
K-E18j	Pack Trainer	LYL	MTL	CE	1	B/Y	B/Y	LBL											[ ] LW
Nmbr	Insignia	Bkgd	Fab	Emb	Tp	Right	Left	Border	CB	GB	PB	GP	LO	LG	WP	WL	LO1	FDL	Misc
K-E19a	PHD CCS	LRD	MTR	CD	1	LGY	LGY	GLD					[ ]						Oversize
K-E19b	PHD CCS	LRD	MTL	CD	1	MGY	MGY	GLD					[ ]						Thin Border
K-E19c	PHD CCS	RED	MTR	CD	3	GRY	GRY	GLD											[ ] PLO Wide Border
K-E19d	PHD CCS	RED	CPW	CD	3	DGY	DGY	GLD						[ ]					[ ] PLG Thin Border
K-E19e	PHD CCS	RED	MTR	CD	3	GRY	GRY	GLD					[ ]						
K-E19f	PHD CCS	LRD	MTL	CD	1	LGY	LGY	LGD	[ ]				[ ]						Thin Border 60° Angle
K-E19g	PHD CCS	LRD	MTR	CD	1	MGY	MGY	LGD					[ ]						Thin Border Thick Knot 30° Angle
K-E19h	PHD CCS	LRD	MTR	CD	1	LGY	LGY	LGD					[ ]						Thin Border
K-E19i	PHD CCS	LRD	CPW	CD	3	MGY	MGY	GLD					[ ]						
K-E19j	PHD CCS	RED	CPW	CD	3	GRY	GRY	GLD						[ ]					
K-E19k	PHD CCS	RED	CPW	CD	1	LGY	LGY	LGD					[ ]						Thin Border
Nmbr	Insignia	Bkgd	Fab	Emb	Tp	Right	Left	Border	CB	GB	PB	GP	LO	LG	WP	WL	LO1	FDL	Misc
K-E20a	Philmont Training	YEL	MTR	CD	1	RED	RED	YEL											[ ] LW Oversize
K-E20b	Philmont Training	YEL	MTL	CD	1	RED	RED	YEL											[ ] LW
K-E20c	Philmont Training	YEL	MTR	CD	1	RED	RED	YEL											[ ] LW
K-E20d	Philmont Training	DYL	MTR	CD	3	RED	RED	DYL											[ ] PLO
K-E20e	Philmont Training	YEL	MTL	CD	1	CAR	CAR	YEL											[ ] LW
K-E20f	Philmont Training	YEL	MTR	CD	1	CAR	CAR	DAF											[ ] LW
Nmbr	Insignia	Bkgd	Fab	Emb	Tp	Right	Left	Border	CB	GB	PB	GP	LO	LG	WP	WL	LO1	FDL	Misc
K-E21a	Unit Leader Award	DBL	MTL	CD	1	MGD	MGD	MGD				[ ]						[ ]	
K-E21b	Unit Leader Award	DBL	MTR	CD	1	DMG	DMG	DMG										[ ]	
K-E21c	Unit Leader Award	DBL	MTR	CD	1	MGD	MGD	MGD										[ ]	Thick Knot
K-E21d	Unit Leader Award	DBL	MTR	CE	1	MGD	MGD	MGD										[ ]	
K-E21e	Unit Leader Award	DBL	MTB	CE	1	DMG	DMG	DMG										[ ]	
Nmbr	Insignia	Bkgd	Fab	Emb	Tp	Right	Left	Border	CB	GB	PB	GP	LO	LG	WP	WL	LO1	FDL	Misc
K-E22a	Alumni Search	LGY	FE	CD	3	BYR	BYR	MGD										[ ]	BM-MTR LBL
K-E22b	Alumni Search	LGY	FE	CD	3	BYR	BYR	MGD										[ ]	BM-MPW MBL
K-E22c	Alumni Search	LGY	FE	CE	3	BYR	BYR	MGD										[ ]	BM-MTL DBL
Nmbr	Insignia	Bkgd	Fab	Emb	Tp	Right	Left	Border	CB	GB	PB	GP	LO	LG	WP	WL	LO1	FDL	Misc
K-E23a	Comm Awd Excel	LRD	MTR	CE	1	LGD	LGD	LGD										[ ]	Oversize / Thick Knot
K-E23b	Comm Awd Excel	RED	MTR	CE	3	GLD	GLD	GLD										[ ]	

Abbreviations

Column Headings (Listed Alphabetically)

Bkgd	Background
Border	Color of Border
CB	Cloth back
Emb	Type of embroidery
Fab	Fabric
FDL	Fleur-de-lis
GB	Gauze back
GP	Gauze plastic back
Insignia	Name of knot
LG	Gauze plastic back with logo
Left	Color for portion of knot to wearer's left
LO	Plastic back with logo
LO1	Plastic back with 100th Anniversary logo
Misc	Additional information
Nmbr	Number and letter for knot
Overhand	Overhand knot (Used for DAM)
PB	Plastic back
Right	Color for portion of knot to wearer's right
Stars & Strips	Used only for the Silver World knot award
Tp	Shape of knot
Trident	Trident instead of knot (Used for Seabadge)
WL	White Plastic with logo
WP	White Plastic

Fabric and Embroidery Abbreviations (Listed Alphabetically)

CD	Computer Design	CTR	Course Twill Right	FTL	Fine Twill Left	MTL	Medium Twill Left
CE	Computer Embroidery	FE	Fully Embroidered	FTR	Fine Twill Right	MTR	Medium Twill Right
CPW	Course Plain Weave	FL	Felt	MPW	Medium Plain Weave	Sw	Swiss Embroidery
CTL	Course Twill Left	FPW	Fine Plain Weave	MTB	Medium Twill Back[46]		

Miscellaneous Abbreviations (Listed Alphabetically)

1LW	100 Logo over White Plastic	LY	Logo over Yellow Plastic	MPB	Milky Plastic Back	PLG	Pelon logo gauze
2010	FDL and 2010 plastic back	MLG	Milky Logo Gauze	MPL	Milky Pelon Logo	PLO	Pelon logo plastic
BM-	Base Material[47]	MLO	Milky Logo	MW1	Milky White w/100 Logo	PW	Plastic over White Plastic
LG1	Gauze Plastic w/100 Logo	MP1	Milky White Pelon w/100	MWP	Milky White Pelon	YL	Plastic over Yellow Plastic
LO1	Plastic Back w/100 Logo	MLW	Milky LW	Pelon	Plastic over Pelon	WP1	White Plastic w/100 Logo
LW	Logo over White Plastic						

Color Abbreviations (Listed Alphabetically)

BGE	Beige	DPG	Deep Green	LBV	Light Blue Violet	PBL	Pale Blue
BGN	Blue Green	DPL	Dark Purple	LGD	Light Gold	PNK	Pink
BLK	Black	DPO	Deep Orange	LGN	Light Green	POR	Pale Orange
BLU	Blue	DPR	Deep Red	LGY	Light Gray	PRD	Pale Red
BOR	Bright Orange	DRD	Dark Red	LKH	Light Khaki	PUR	Purple
BRN	Brown	DSG	Dark Silver Gray	LMG	Light Metallic Gold	PYL	Pale Yellow
BGN	Blue Green	DST	Dark Steel Gray	LOR	Light Orange	RBL	Royal Blue
BVI	Blue Violet	DSV	Dark Silver	LPR	Light Purple	RED	Red
BYL	Bright Yellow	DTN	Dark Tan	LRD	Light Red	RGY	Rose Gray
BYR	Blue-Yellow-Red	DVI	Dark Violet	LSG	Light Silver Gray	ROS	Rose
B/Y	Blue, Yellow	DYG	Dark Yellow Green	LST	Light Steel Gray	RWB	Red, White, Blue
CAN	Canary	DYL	Dark Yellow	LTN	Light Tan	R/W	Red and White
CAR	Candy Apple Red	ECR	Ecru	LYL	Light Yellow	SBL	Sky Blue
CSK	Corn Silk	EGS	Eggshell	MBL	Medium Blue	SFL	Sunflower
DAF	Daffodil	FGN	Forest Green	MBN	Medium Brown	SGD	Star Gold
DBG	Dark Beige	GGN	Gold Green	MGD	Metallic Gold	SGY	Silver Gray
DBL	Dark Blue	GGR	Gold, Green, Red	MGY	Medium Gray	SIL	Silver
DBN	Dark Brown	GLD	Gold	MLV	Medium Lavender	SMY	Silver Mylar
DGR	Dark Blue Green	GRB	Green, Red, Blue	MNB	Mid-Night Blue	SNW	Snow White
DBV	Dark Blue Violet	GRN	Green	MNG	Mid-Night Gray	STG	Steel Gray
DGD	Dark Gold	GRY	Gray	MPR	Medium Purple	TAN	Tan
DGN	Dark Green	G/W	Green, White	MRD	Medium Red	VIO	Violet
DGY	Dark Gray	IVO	Ivory	MSV	Metallic Silver	WBG	White, Blue, Green
DLV	Dark Lavender	KGN	Kelly Green	MTD	Mustard	WHT	White
DMG	Dark Metallic Gold	KHA	Khaki	MYL	Medium Yellow	WLG	Woodland Green
DMS	Dark Metallic Silver	LAV	Lavender	NBL	Navy Blue	W/R	White and Red
DOL	Dark Olive	LBG	Light Beige	OLV	Olive	YEL	Yellow
DOR	Dark Orange	LBL	Light Blue	ORG	Orange	YGN	Yellow Green
DPB	Deep Blue	LBN	Light Brown	OWT	Off White		

Note: Ranges of colors are listed for an individual knot to depict variations. For example, this enables us to list color variations of RED, LRD, and DRD for the K-A02 (Heroism) knot. The Red listed in that knot may not match red in the K-B02 (Silver Buffalo) knot. It does however provide a basis for color variations within an individual knot.

Disclaimer

The Listing of Knot Issues is as complete as my research has been able to document. I am aware that it may not be complete and welcome additional information. Please contact me if you have a knot award that is different than those listed.

---

[46] Knot is sewn on the backside of the twill material. It has some appearance of both Twill and Weave.

[47] Base Material is only used for fully embroidered knots. "BM-" is followed by the type of material (ie., FTR).

Twill Patterns [48]

Fine Twill

Medium Twill [49]

Coarse Twill

Weave Paterns [50]

Fine Plain Weave

Medium Plain Weave

Coarse Plain Weave

Medium Twill Back

Note: The Medium Twill Back is shown in 2 angles. The knot is sewn on the back side of the twill, which the light twill can be easily noticed when the knot is held at a 45 degree angle. The twill could be right or left. We have decided not to differentiate between the two. In the case of the shown knot, the twill is angled left.

To see a scan of the front of each knot listed in the Listing of Knot Awards (K-List), go to web site: *http://www.crowl.org/George/* Reference: Varieties of Official BSA Square Knots.

---

[48] There are 3 distinct patterns for Twills. The determining bases for the twills are as follows: A Fine Twill has 10 (± 1) valleys per 5 mm. Medium Twill has 7 (± 1) valleys per 5 mm. Coarse Twill has 5 (± 1) valleys per 5 mm. A collector should be able to look at the knot and determine which twill is used and not have to measure it. Simply use the knots shown above to determine if it is a Fine, Medium, or Coarse Twill.

[49] The top Medium Twill was produced up though the 1980's. The bottom Medium Twill is the style that is currently being produced.

[50] Plain weaves have three distinct patterns. The determining basis for the weaves, are as follows: A Fine Plain Weave has 10 straight threads (± 1) per 5 mm X 17 +, over 1 under 1 thread count per 5 mm. A Medium Plain Weave has 10 straight threads (± 1) per 5 mm X 10 (± 1) over 1 under 1-thread count per 5 mm. A Coarse Plain Weave has than 9 straight threads per 5 mm X 11-13 over 1 under 1-thread counts per 5 mm. A collector should be able to look at the knot and determine which weave is used and not have to measure it. Simply use the knots shown above to determine if it is a Fine Medium, or Coarse Weave.

Rearrangement of knots from the 6th Edition

To align the knots based on both when they were manufactured and by specific background color, a rearrangement of the order was accomplished some of the named knots. All knots were not rearranged. The knots that were changed are listed below with the changes.

Honor Medal

Knot	From	Knot	From	Knot	From	Knot	From	Knot	From
K-A01a	K-A01a	K-A01b	Added	K-A01c	K-A01b	K-A01d	Added	K-A01e	K-A01c
K-A01f	K-A01d	K-A01g	Added	K-A01h	Added	K-A01i	Added	K-A01j	Added
K-A01k	Added	K-A01l	Added	K-A01m	Added	K-A01n	Added	K-A01o	K-A01e
K-A01p	Added	K-A01q	K-A01j	K-A01r	Added	K-A01s	K-A01f	K-A01t	K-A01h
K-A01u	Added	K-A01v	K-A01k	K-A01w	Added	K-A01x	K-A01i	K-A01y	Added
K-A01z	Added	K-A01aa	K-A01l	K-A01ae	K-A01g	K-A01ab	Added	K-A01ac	Added
K-A01ad	Added	K-A01af	Added	K-A01ag	Added	K-A01ah	Added	K-A01ai	Added

Heroism Award

Knot	From	Knot	From	Knot	From	Knot	From	Knot	From
K-A02a	K-A02a	K-A02b	K-A02b	K-A02c	Added	K-A02d	K-A02c	K-A02e	K-A02d
K-A02f	K-A02e	K-A02g	K-A01i	K-A01h	K-A02f	K-A01i	K-A01h	K-A02j	Added
K-A02k	K-A02g	K-A02l	Added	K-A02m	Added	K-A02n	Added		

Medal of Merit

Knot	From	Knot	From	Knot	From	Knot	From	Knot	From
K-A03a	K-C03a	K-A03b	K-C03b	K-A03c	K-C03c	K-A03d	K-C03d	K-A03e	K-C03e
K-A03f	K-C03f	K-A03g	K-C03g	K-A03h	K-C03h	K-A03i	Added	K-A03j	K-C03i
K-A03k	K-C03j	K-A03l	K-C03k	K-A03m	K-C03l	K-A03n	Added	K-A03o	K-C03m
K-A03p	K-C03n	K-A03q	K-C03o	K-A03r	Added	K-A03s	Added	K-A03t	Added
K-A03u	Added	K-A03v	Added	K-A03w	Added				

Silver World

Knot	From	Knot	From	Knot	From	Knot	From	Knot	From
K-B01a	K-B01a	K-B01d	K-B01d	K-B01f	K-B01e	K-B01h	K-B01g	K-B01j	Added
K-B01b	K-B01b	K-B01e	Added	K-B01g	K-B01f	K-B01i	Added	K-B01k	Added
K-B01c	K-B01c								

Silver Buffalo

Knot	From	Knot	From	Knot	From	Knot	From	Knot	From
K-B02a	K-B02a	K-B02b	K-B02b	K-B02c	Added	K-B02d	Added	K-B02e	Added
K-B02f	Added	K-B02g	Added	K-B02h	K-B02c	K-B02i	K-B02d	K-B02j	Added
K-B02k	Added	K-B02l	Added	K-B02m	K-B02e	K-B02n	K-B02g	K-B02o	K-B02f
K-B02p	K-B02 m	K-B02q	K-B02j	K-B02r	K-B02h	K-B02s	Added	K-B02t	Added
K-B02u	K-C02i	K-B02v	K-C02l	K-B02w	Added	K-B02x	Added	K-B02y	K-B02k
K-B02z	Added	K-B02aa	Added	K-B02ab	Added	K-B02ac	Added		

Silver Antelope

Knot	From	Knot	From	Knot	From	Knot	From	Knot	From
K-B03a	K-B03a	K-B03b	K-B03b	K-B03c	Added	K-B03d	Added	K-B03e	K-B03c
K-B03f	Added	K-B03g	K-B03d	K-B03h	K-B03e	K-B03i	Added	K-B03j	Added
K-B03k	K-B03j	K-B03l	Added	K-B03m	Added	K-B03n	K-B03f	K-B03o	Added
K-B03p	K-B03i	K-B03q	Added	K-B03r	Added	K-B03s	K-B03h	K-B03t	K-B03g
K-B03u	Added	K-B03v	K-B03l	K-B03w	K-B03m	K-B03x	Added	K-B03y	Added
K-B03z	Added	K-B03aa	K-B03p	K-B03ab	Added	K-B03ac	K-B03k	K-B03ad	K-B03n
K-B03ae	Added	K-B03af	K-B03r	K-B03ag	K-B03q	K-B03ah	K-B03o	K-B03ai	K-B03s
K-B03aj	Added	K-B03ak	Added	K-B03al	Added	K-B03am	Added	K-B03an	Added
K-B03ao	Added	K-B03ap	Added						

Silver Beaver

Knot	From	Knot	From	Knot	From	Knot	From	Knot	From
K-B04a	K-B04a	K-B04b	K-B04b	K-B04c	Added	K-B04d	Added	K-B04e	Added
K-B04f	Added	K-B04g	K-B04c	K-B04h	K-B04e	K-B04i	Added	K-B04j	K-B04f
K-B04k	Added	K-B04l	K-B04g	K-B04m	K-B04d	K-B04n	Added	K-B04o	K-B04h
K-B04p	Added	K-B04q	K-B04i	K-B04r	K-B04ad	K-B04s	K-B04j	K-B04t	Added
K-B04u	Added	K-B04v	Added	K-B04w	Added	K-B04x	K-B04k	K-B04y	K-B04m
K-B04z	K-B04n	K-B04aa	Added	K-B04ab	K-B04l	K-B04ac	Added	K-B04ad	K-B04o
K-B04ae	K-B04x	K-B04af	Added	K-B04ag	Added	K-B04ah	Added	K-B04ai	Added
K-B04aj	K-B04p	K-B04ak	K-B04q	K-B04al	K-B04r	K-B04am	K-B04s	K-B04an	K-B04t
K-B04ao	Added	K-B04ap	K-B04u	K-B04aq	Added	K-B04ar	K-B04aa	K-B04as	K-B04y
K-B04at	K-B04z	K-B04au	Added	K-B04av	K-B04v	K-B04aw	K-B04w	K-B04ax	K-B04ab
K-B04ay	Added	K-B04az	Added	K-B04ba	Added	K-B04bb	Added	K-B04bc	Added
K-B04bd	Added	K-B04be	Added	K-B04bf	Added	K-B04bg	Added	K-B04bh	Added
K-B04bi	Added	K-B04bj	K-B04ac	K-B04bk	Added				

District Award of Merit

Knot	From	Knot	From	Knot	From	Knot	From	Knot	From
K- B05a	K- B05a	K- B05b	K- B05b	K- B05c	K- B05c	K- B05d	K-B05d	K-B05e	K-B05e
K- B05f	K-B05f	K-B05g	K-B05g	K-B05h	K-B05h	K-B05i	K-B05i	K-B05j	K-B05j
K-B05k	K-B05r	K-B05l	K-B05k	K-B05m	K-B05l	K-B05n	K-B05s	K-B05o	K-B05m
K-B05p	K-B05n	K-B05q	K-B05o	K-B05r	Added	K-B05s	Added	K-B05t	Added
K-B05u	Added								

Order of the Arrow Distinguished Service Award

Knot	From	Knot	From	Knot	From	Knot	From	Knot	From
K-B06a	K-B06a	K- B06b	K-B06b	K- B06c	K-B06f	K- B06d	K-B06d	K-B03e	K-B06b
K-B03f	Added	K-B03g	K-B06k	K-B03h	K-B06g	K-B03i	K-B06i	K-B03j	Added
K-B03k	K-B06g	K-B03l	K-B06b	K-B03m	Added	K-B03n	Added	K-B03o	Added
K-B03p	Added	K-B03q	Added						

Eagle Scout Award

Knot	From	Knot	From	Knot	From	Knot	From	Knot	From
K-C01a	K-C01a	K-C01b	Added	K-C01c	K-C01c	K-C01d	K-C01b	K-C01e	Added
K-C01f	Added	K-C01g	Added	K-C01h	Added	K-C01i	Added	K-C01j	Added
K-C01k	K-C01d	K-C01l	Added	K-C01m	K-C01e	K-C01n	K-C01f	K-C01o	Added
K-C01p	Added	K-C01q	K-C01g	K-C01r	Added	K-C01s	K-C01i	K-C01t	Added
K-C01u	K-C01j	K-C01v	Added	K-C01w	K-C01k	K-C01x	Added	K-C01y	Added
K-C01z	Added	K-C01aa	K-C01l	K-C01aa	Added	K-C01ab	K-C01p	K-C01ac	K-C01r
K-C01ad	K-C01t	K-C01ae	Added	K-C01af	K-C01m	K-C01ag	K-C01n	K-C01ah	K-C01o
K-C01ai	K-C01q	K-C01at	Added	K-C01aj	K-C01s	K-C01ak	Added	K-C01al	Added
K-C01am	Added	K-C01an	Added	K-C01ao	Added	K-C01ap	K-C01t	K-C01aq	K-C01v
K-C01ar	K-C01w	K-C01as	Added	K-C01au	Added	K-C01av	Added	K-C01aw	K-C01u
K-C01ax	Added	K-C01ay	Added	K-C01az	Added	K-C01ba	Added	K-C01bb	Added
K-C01bc	Added	K-C01bd	Added						

Quartermaster Award

Knot	From	Knot	From	Knot	From	Knot	From	Knot	From
K-C02a	Added	K-C02b	K-C02a	K-C02c	K-C02b	K-C02d	K-C02f	K-C02e	K-C02d
K-C02f	K-C02b	K-C02g	Added	K-C02h	Added	K-C02i	K-C02k	K-C02j	K-C02g
K-C02k	K-C062i	K-C02l	Added	K-C02m	K-C02g	K-C02n	K-C02b	K-C02o	Added
K-C02p	Added	K-C02q	Added	K-C02r	Added	K-C02s	Added	K-C02t	Added
K-C02u	Added	K-C02v	Added						

Explorer Achievement Award

Knot	From	Knot	From	Knot	From	Knot	From	Knot	From
K-C06a	K-C06c	K-C06b	K-C06b	K-C06c	K-C06a	K-C06d	Added	K-C06e	K-C06k
K-C06f	Added	K-C06g	K-C06d	K-C06h	K-C06l	K-C06i	Added	K-C06j	Added
K-C06k	K-C06e	K-C06l	K-C06n	K-C06m	K-C06j	K-C06n	K-C06l	K-C06o	Added
K-C06p	Added	K-C06q	Added	K-C06r	Added	K-C06s	K-C06f	K-C06t	Added
K-C06u	K-C06g	K-C06v	K-C06h	K-C06w	K-C06i	K-C06x	K-C06l	K-C06y	Added
K-C06z	K-C06m	K-C06aa	Added	K-C06ab	K-C06j	K-C06ac	Added	K-C06ad	Added
K-C06ae	Added	K-C06af	Added						

Arrow of Light

Knot	From	Knot	From	Knot	From	Knot	From	Knot	From
K-C07a	K-C07f	K-C07b	Added	K-C07c	K-C07p	K-C07d	Added	K-C07e	Added
K-C07f	K-C07a	K-C07g	Added	K-C07h	K-C07g	K-C07i	Added	K-C07j	Added
K-C07k	Added	K-C07l	Added	K-C07m	Added	K-C07n	Added	K-C07o	Added
K-C07p	K-C07h	K-C07q	Added	K-C07r	K-C07s	K-C07s	Added	K-C07u	Added
K-C07t	Added	K-C07v	Added	K-C07w	Added	K-C07x	Added	K-C07y	K-C07d
K-C07z	K-C07c	K-C07aa	K-C07e	K-C07ab	Added	K-C07ac	K-C07q	K-C07ad	K-C07b
K-C07ae	Added	K-C07af	Added	K-C07ag	K-C07o	K-C07ah	Added	K-C07ai	Added
K-C07aj	Added	K-C07ak	Added	K-C07al	K-C07m	K-C07am	Added	K-C07an	K-C07l
K-C07ao	K-C07i	K-C07ap	K-C07n	K-C07aq	K-C07k	K-C07ar	K-C07j	K-C07as	Added
K-C07at	K-C07r	K-C07au	Added	K-C07av	Added	K-C07aw	Added	K-C07ax	Added
K-C07ay	Added	K-C07az	Added	K-C07ba	Added	K-C07bb	Added	K-C07bc	Added
K-C07bd	Added	K-C07be	Added	K-C07bf	Added	K-C07bg	Added	K-C07bh	Added
K-C07bi	Added	K-C07bj	Added	K-C07bk	Added	K-C07bl	Added	K-C07bm	Added
K-C07bn	Added	K-C07bo	Added	K-C07bp	Added	K-C07bq	Added	K-C07br	Added
K-C07bs	Added								

Venturing Silver Award

Knot	From	Knot	From	Knot	From	Knot	From	Knot	From
K-C09a	K-C09a	K-C09b	Added	K-C09c	K-C09b	K-C09d	K-C09c	K-C09e	K-C09d
K-C09f	Added	K-C09g	K-C09d	K-C09h	Added	K-C09i	Added		

James E. West

Knot	From	Knot	From	Knot	From	Knot	From	Knot	From
K-C10a	K-C10b	K-C10b	Added	K-C10c	K-C10b	K-C10d	K-C10m	K-C10e	Added
K-C10f	K-C10k	K-C10g	Added	K-C10h	Added	K-C10i	K-C10d	K-C10j	Added
K-C10k	K-C10g	K-C10l	K-C10a	K-C10m	K-C10e	K-C10n	K-C10j	K-C10o	K-C10o
K-C10p	Added	K-C10q	K-C10i	K-C10r	Added	K-C10s	K-C10h	K-C10t	Added
K-C10u	Added	K-C10v	K-C10l	K-C10w	K-C10c	K-C10x	K-C10n	K-C10y	K-C10f
K-C10z	Added	K-C10aa	Added	K-C10ab	Added	K-C10ac	Added		

Youth Religious Award

Knot	From	Knot	From	Knot	From	Knot	From	Knot	From
K-D01a	K-D01a	K-D01b	K-D01b	K-D01c	K-D01c	K-D01d	K-D01d	K-D01e	K-D01e
K-D01f	K-D01f	K-D01g	K-D01g	K-D01h	Added	K-D01i	Added	K-D01j	K-D01h
K-D01k	K-D01i	K-D01l	K-D01j	K-D01m	K-D01k	K-D01n	K-D01l	K-D01o	K-D01m
K-D01p	K-D01n	K-D01q	Added						

Adult Religious Award

Knot	From	Knot	From	Knot	From	Knot	From	Knot	From
K-D02a	K-D02a	K-D02b	K-D02b	K-D02c	K-D02c	K-D02d	Added	K-D02e	K-D02k
K-D02f	Added	K-D02g	Added	K-D02h	Added	K-D02i	Added	K-D02j	K-D02f
K-D02k	Added	K-D02l	K-D02j	K-D02m	K-D02h	K-D02n	Added	K-D02o	K-D02i
K-D02p	Added	K-D02q	Added	K-D02r	K-D02d	K-D02s	K-D02e	K-D02t	Added
K-D02u	Added	K-D02v	Added	K-D02w	Added	K-D02x	Added	K-D02y	Added
K-D02z	K-D02g	K-D02aa	Added	K-D02ab	Added	K-D02ac	Added	K-D02ad	Added
K-D02ae	Added	K-D02af	Added	K-D02ag	Added	K-D02ah	Added	K-D02ai	Added

Scouter's Key

Knot	From	Knot	From	Knot	From	Knot	From	Knot	From
K-E01a	K-E01a	K-E01b	Added	K-E01c	K-E01b	K-E01d	K-E01v	K-E01e	K-E01c
K-E01f	Added	K-E01g	Added	K-E01h	Added	K-E01i	Added	K-E01j	K-E01d
K-E01k	K-E01e	K-E01l	Added	K-E01m	K-E01f	K-E01n	K-E01g	K-E01o	Added
K-E01p	Added	K-E01q	K-E01h	K-E01r	Added	K-E01s	K-E01i	K-E01t	K-E01l
K-E01u	Added	K-E01v	K-E01k	K-E01w	Added	K-E01x	K-E01j	K-E01y	K-E01n
K-E01z	Added	K-E01aa	Added	K-E01ab	K-E01o	K-E01ac	K-E01m	K-E01ad	K-E01v
K-E01ae	K-E01w	K-E01af	K-E01p	K-E01ag	K-E01q	K-E01ah	K-E01r	K-E01ai	K-E01s
K-E01aj	K-E01u	K-E01ak	Added	K-E01al	Added	K-E01am	Added		

Scouter's Training Award

Knot	From	Knot	From	Knot	From	Knot	From	Knot	From
K-E02a	K-E02a	K-E02b	Added	K-E02c	Added	K-E02d	K-E02b	K-E02e	K-E02c
K-E02f	Added	K-E02g	Added	K-E02h	Added	K-E02i	K-E02d	K-E02j	K-E02e
K-E02k	Added	K-E02l	Added	K-E02m	Added	K-E02n	Added	K-E02o	Added
K-E02p	K-E02z	K-E02q	K-E02f	K-E02r	Added	K-E02s	K-E02aa	K-E02t	Added
K-E02u	Added	K-E02v	K-E02g	K-E02w	K-E02h	K-E02x	Added	K-E02y	K-E02i
K-E02z	K-E02j	K-E02aa	Added	K-E02ab	K-E02k	K-E02ac	K-E02l	K-E02ad	K-E02n
K-E02ae	K-E02m	K-E02af	Added	K-E02ag	Added	K-E02ah	Added	K-E02ai	Added
K-E02aj	Added	K-E02ak	Added	K-E02al	Added	K-E02am	K-E02o	K-E02an	K-E02p
K-E02ao	K-E02q	K-E02ap	Added	K-E02aq	K-E02r	K-E02ar	Added	K-E02as	K-E02s
K-E02at	Added	K-E02au	K-E02t	K-E02av	Added	K-E02w	Added	K-E02ax	Added
K-E02ay	Added	K-E02az	K-E02u	K-E02ba	K-E02v	K-E02bb	Added	K-E02bc	Added
K-E02bd	Added	K-E02be	Added	K-E02bf	K-E02x	K-E02bg	K-E02w	K-E02bh	Added
K-E02bi	Added	K-E02bj	Added	K-E02bk	Added	K-E02bl	Added	K-E02bm	K-E02y
K-E02bn	Added	K-E02bo	Added	K-E02bp	Added	K-E02bq	Added	K-E02br	K-E02ab
K-E02bs	K-E02ac	K-E02bt	Added	K-E02bu	K-E02ad	K-E02bv	Added	K-E02bw	Added

Scoutmaster Award of Merit

Knot	From	Knot	From	Knot	From	Knot	From	Knot	From
K-E12a	Added	K-E12b	K-E12a	K-E12c	K-E12b	K-E12d	K-E12k	K-E12e	K-E12e
K-E12f	K-E12f	K-E12g	K-E12d	K-E12h	K-E12i	K-E12i	K-E12c	K-E12j	Added
K-E12k	K-E12g	K-E12l	Added	K-E12m	Added	K-E12n	Added	K-E12o	Added
K-E12p	Added								

Distinguished Commissioner

Knot	From	Knot	From	Knot	From	Knot	From	Knot	From
K-E13a	K-E13a	K-E13b	K-E13b	K-E13c	K-E13d	K-E13d	K-E13g	K-E13e	Added
K-E13f	Added	K-E13g	Added	K-E13h	Added	K-E13i	K-E13c	K-E13j	K-E13e
K-E13k	Added	K-E13l	K-E13f	K-E13m	Added	K-E13n	Added	K-E13o	Added
K-E13p	Added								

Professional Training Award

Knot	From	Knot	From	Knot	From	Knot	From	Knot	From
K-E06a	K-E06a	K-E06b	K-E06a	K-E06c	K-E06c	K-E06d	K-E06f	K-E06e	K-E06e
K-E06f	Added	K-E06h	Added	K-E06g	K-E06d	K-E06i	Added		

Cubmaster Award

Knot	From	Knot	From	Knot	From	Knot	From	Knot	From
K-E07a	K-E07a	K-E07b	K-E07b	K-E07c	K-E07f	K-E07d	K-E07g	K-E07e	Added
K-E07f	Added	K-E07g	K-E07h	K-E07h	K-E07j	K-E07i	K-E07c	K-E07j	K-E07d
K-E07k	K-E07i	K-E07l	K-E07k	K-E07m	Added	K-E07n	Added	K-E07o	Added
K-E07p	K-E07e	K-E07q	Added	K-E07r	Added				

Den Leader Coach Award

Knot	From	Knot	From	Knot	From	Knot	From	Knot	From
K-E08a	K-E08a	K-E08b	K-E08b	K-E08c	K-E08c	K-E08d	K-E08d	K-E08e	K-E08e
K-E08f	K-E08f	K-E08g	K-E08l	K-E08h	Added	K-E08i	K-E08m	K-E08n	K-E08j
K-E08j	K-E08k	K-E08k	K-E08g	K-E08l	K-E08h	K-E08m	K-E08i	K-E08o	K-E08n
K-E08p	Added	K-E08q	Added						

Den Leader Award

Knot	From	Knot	From	Knot	From	Knot	From	Knot	From
K-E10a	K-E10a	K-E10b	Added	K-E10c	Added	K-E10d	K-E10g	K-E10e	K-E10b
K-E10f	K-E10c	K-E10g	K-E10d	K-E10h	K-E10e	K-E10i	K-E10f	K-E10j	K-E10h
K-E10k	Added	K-E10l	Added	K-E10m	Added	K-E10n	Added	K-E10o	Added
K-E10p	Added	K-E10q	Added	K-E10r	Added	K-E10s	Added	K-E10t	Added

Cub Scouter Award

Knot	From	Knot	From	Knot	From	Knot	From	Knot	From
K-E11a	K-E11a	K-E11b	K-E11b	K-E11c	K-E11c	K-E11d	K-E11d	K-E11e	K-E11e
K-E11f	K-E11f	K-E11g	K-E11g	K-E11h	K-E11j	K-E11i	K-E11m	K-E11j	K-E11i
K-E11k	K-E11	K-E11l	Added	K-E11m	Added	K-E11n	K-E11h	K-E11o	Added
K-E11p	Added	K-E11q	Added	K-E11r	Added	K-E11s	Added	K-E11t	Added
K-E11u	K-E11k	K-E11v	Added	K-E11w	Added				

Tiger Cub Den Leader Award

Knot	From	Knot	From	Knot	From	Knot	From	Knot	From
K-E15a	K-E15a	K-E15b	K-E15b	K-E15c	K-E15j	K-E15d	K-E15p	K-E15e	K-E15e
K-E15f	K-E15f	K-E15g	Added	K-E15h	K-E15l	K-E15i	K-E15o	K-E15j	K-E15m
K-E15k	K-E15d	K-E15l	Added	K-E15m	K-E15i	K-E15n	Added	K-E15o	Added
K-E15p	Added	K-E15q	K-E15k	K-E15r	Added	K-E15s	Added	K-E15t	K-E15g
K-E15u	Added	K-E15v	Added	K-E15w	K-E15n	K-E15x	K-E15q	K-E15y	K-E15h
K-E15z	Added	K-E15aa	Added	K-E15ab	Added	K-E15ac	Added	K-E15ad	K-E15c
K-E15ae	Added	K-E15af	Added	K-E15ag	Added	K-E15ah	Added	K-E15ai	Added
K-E15aj	Added								

Pack Trainer Award

Knot	From	Knot	From	Knot	From	Knot	From	Knot	From
K-E18a	K-E18a	K-E18b	K-E18b	K-E18c	K-E18c	K-E18d	K-E18d	K-E18e	K-E18e
K-E18f	Added	K-E18g	K-E18f	K-E18h	K-E18g	K-E18i	Added		

PHD College of Commissioner Science

Knot	From	Knot	From	Knot	From	Knot	From	Knot	From
K-E19a	K-E19a	K-E19b	K-E19b	K-E19c	K-E19c	K-E19d	K-E19d	K-E19e	K-E19e
K-E19f	Added	K-E19g	K-E19f	K-E19h	K-E19g	K-E19i	Added	K-E19j	Added
K-E19j	Added								

Illustrations

Type of Knot

Tp	Example of style of knot	Description
0a		The Silver World is the only knot award issued with stars and stripes and a globe with stars in the center.
0b		This is similar to the 0a above. The size of the globe is different, and the knot has a smaller overall size.
1		The shape of this knot, if held sideways, looks like an "S". This was original and standard shape for most knot issues.
2		There are only a few knots issued with this shape. The basic shape of this knot resembles a pair of "H's" when held sideways. The ends of this knot are pointed inward.
3		The shape of this knot is similar to type 2 knot. The ends are pointed up on the right and down on the left as worn, similar to the type 1 knot.
4		The George Meany knot is the only type 4 knot. It is slightly different than a type 3 knot in shape. The ends are blunt with no points. The ends on the right side (as viewed) turn downward.
5		The original Spurgeon knot has a unique shape. This is the only knot award with this shaped square knot.
6		The Boyce knot is the only one with this shape.
7		This was only used on the Pack Trainer misprint that was recalled by National Supply.
10		The District Award of Merit is the only knot award in the shape of an overhand knot.

Tp	Example of style of knot	Description
11		The Seabadge is the only knot award with a trident instead of a square knot. The outer portions of the trident are curved.
12		The outer portion of this trident is straight.
13		This is a very thick embroidered trident. The outer portions are very curved.
14		This is a very thick embroidered trident. The outer portions are slightly curved.

Back of Knots

Knots have been issued with a number of different backing materials. Some of these have had a number of different styles for the same listing in the above table. This will help define the various types of backs used on knot awards.

CB - Cloth back

There is no extra added material, or may have a gum or glue on the back.

GB - Gauze back

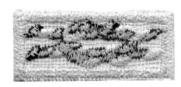

The knot is sewn on material that is backed by gauze. There are variations in the gauze material.

PB - Plastic back

Plastic is molded to the knot and is shinny.

Plastic is dull and flat on the surface.

There are two varieties of this type, one is completely flat, and the other has a screen impression.

GP – Gauze plastic back

Gauze is used in the sewing process and then plastic is molded to back of the knot. This type has a shinny plastic back.

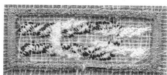

Same as above, except the plastic is flat on and dull.

LO - Logo plastic back

Molded, shinny, plastic back with supply division logo on the plastic.

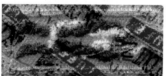

Plastic is dull and flat with a logo imprinted on plastic.

LG - Logo gauze plastic back

Dull flat plastic with standard logo.

Logo gauze plastic back

Dull flat plastic with yellow logo.

WP - White plastic back

Backing is white.

White plastic on knot prior to the logo being used by the BSA has this general appearance.

WL - White plastic back with logo

White plastic with logo.

CD knots that were made in the 2000's with white plastic have the logo backing.

LO1 - Logo plastic back with 100th anniversary logo

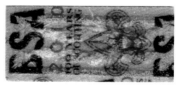

Plastic back with 100th anniversary logo.

 The plastic back with 100th anniversary logo is placed on the back of the knot in a different layout.

FDL - Fleur-de-Lis

 Plastic back with Fleur de Lis and "Since 1910" logo.

Miscellaneous

The following knot backs are listed in the miscellaneous column.

BLU PB – Blue plastic back

 Backing has a shiny blue plastic.

 Backing has a dull blue plastic.

LBL PB - Light blue plastic back

 Backing is dull light blue similar to a white plastic back.

PBL PB - Pale blue plastic back

 Backing is pale blue similar to a white plastic back.

GRY PB – Gray plastic back

 Backing has a gray plastic back.

DGY PB – Dark Gray plastic back

 Backing has a dark gray plastic back.

GRN LO – Green logo plastic back

Logo plastic back with a green tint.

IVO PB – Ivory plastic back

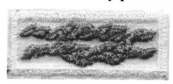

Backing has an ivory appearance.

MLK PB – Milky plastic back

Backing has a milky appearance.

RED PB – Red plastic back

Plastic backing has a red appearance.

DRD PB – Dark Red plastic back

Plastic backing has a dark red appearance.

YEL PB – Yellow plastic back

Backing has a light yellow appearance.

Pelon – Pelon plastic back

Pelon is used for the backing with plastic over it.

PW – Plastic over white plastic

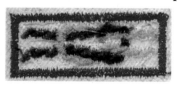

Backing has a clear plastic over the both the white plastic and the stitching.

LW – Logo plastic over white plastic

 Backing is clear plastic with the Scout Shop logo over white plastic. You can see the back of the stitching over the white plastic, which is used as a base.

LY - Logo plastic over yellow plastic

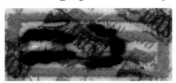 Backing is clear plastic with the Scout Shop logo over light yellow plastic. You can see the back of the stitching over the light yellow plastic, which is used as a base.

MLO - Milky plastic with the Scout Shop logo

 Backing is a milky plastic with the Scout Shop logo.

MLG - Milky plastic with the Scout Shop logo over gauze

 Backing is a milky plastic with the Scout Shop logo over gauze.

MLW - Milky plastic with the Scout Shop logo over white plastic

 Backing is a milky plastic with the Scout Shop logo over white plastic.

MPL - Milky plastic with the Scout Shop logo over Pelon

 Backing is a milky plastic with the Scout Shop logo over Pelon.

MWG - Milky white logo plastic over gauze

 Backing is a milky plastic with the Scout Shop logo over gauze.

PLG - Clear plastic with the Scout Shop logo over Pelon and Gauze

 Backing is a milky plastic with the Scout Shop logo over Pelon and gauze. The gauze is visible over the Pelon.

PLO – Clear plastic with the Scout Shop logo over Pelon

Pelon is used under the plastic with the BSA logo.

This has a flat plastic backing.

1LW - Plastic back with 100th anniversary logo over white plastic

Backing is a clear plastic with the 100th anniversary logo over white plastic.

MP1 - Milky plastic back with 100th anniversary logo over Pelon

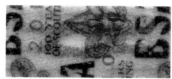

Backing is a milky white plastic with the 100th anniversary logo over Pelon.

MW1 – Milky White plastic with 100th anniversary logo

Backing is a milky white plastic with the 100th anniversary logo.

PL1 - Plastic back with 100th anniversary logo over Pelon

Backing is a clear plastic with the 100th anniversary logo over Pelon.

WP1 - White plastic with 100th anniversary logo

Backing is a white plastic with the 100th anniversary logo..

LG1 - Gauze plastic with 100th anniversary logo

Backing is a clear plastic with the 100th anniversary logo over gauze.

2010 - Plastic back with a 2010 Logo

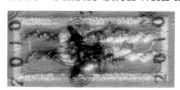

Plastic back with a 2010 logo. Note: This back does not have "BSA" on the plastic back.

How to use the K-Listing

At the request of many collectors, this section is devoted to the collecting of knot awards. The above listing is a complete list of all knots issued by name, color, material, border, knot color, and backing at the time of publication. If there are others, we do not know of them. Keep in mind that new variations are constantly being produced. This list will be updated as time goes by.

George Crowl maintains a visual of the Knot listing for collectors at *__http://www.crowl.org/George/__* Square Knot Varieties. This is a great source to see a scan of every line item in the K-List.

There are 17 knots that are no longer produced – Air Scout/Explorer Ace, Cubmaster Award, Cub Scouter Award, Den Leader Coach's Award (prior to 1988), Den Leader Coach Award, Explorer Achievement Award (also known as Silver Award 2), Explorer Silver Award (Type 1), Heroism Award, Pack Trainer Award,. Ranger Award, Scoutmaster Award of Merit, Seabadge, Skipper's Key, Speaker Bank, Spurgeon Award, Tiger Cub Den Leader Award, Webelos Den Leader Award.

You will need to decide how you want to collect knots. Collections can be categorized into the following areas: Simple, Basic, Standard, and Complete collection. This will help you in deciding which type of collection you desire, and how to use this listing.

Simple Collection

A Simple collection will include one (1) knot from each alphanumeric listed knot. You would collect one knot from the category listed as K-A01, K-A02, K-A03, K-B01, etc. It would not matter which one of the small letters you have. It would be easy to collect the current edition of each knot (by name). This would amount to a total of 53 (knots listed by name) that have been produced over the years.

Basic Collection

A Basic collection is going to be the most common. It includes all major color changes for the listed knot and knot type. I will use the Eagle Scout knot as an example. You would collect one knot with a khaki background (K-C01a through K-C01j). The type of twill is not important in this collection. Next would be a blue background knot (K- C01k through K-C01o). Followed by a white background knot (K-C01p through K-C01t). Add one of the green background knots (K-C01u through K-C01x). All remaining knots are on a beige background. The first two of these (K- C01y through K-C01bd) have brown borders, which only one is needed. The remaining knots have either beige, light beige, or tan border. You only need one of the beige and one of either light beige or tan border. This collection will provide all the primary colors for the knots. The type of backing does not matter. This will provide a great visual collection. This is the type of display I made for talking about knot awards. I use my display to show the type awards that can be earned/awarded and a history of knot awards.

This collection would be complete with 115 knots. If misprints are also included, then add 19 additional knots are needed.

NOTE: This is the type of collection that I recommend for collectors.

Standard Collection

A Standard collection would include one of every type of front by type of twill/weave, and color changes. This is a more in-depth collection than the basic collection. You would have one knot for each line listed. An example would be to have one knot for each of the Honor medal knots listed (example: K-A01a through K-A01ai. The back of the knot is not important, as only the front of the knot is displayed. At present time, we have identified 1041 knots needed to complete this collection

Complete Collection

A Complete collection will include all listed items to include all backs. This collection will only be for a few dedicated collectors. At time of publication, 1,258 varieties of knots (including the front and backs) have been identified to complete this collection. There are new varieties found every month. This type of collection is only for the dedicated collector.

Listing of Knot Device Issues [51]

Nmbr	Insignia	Dates	Characteristics	S	M	MB	ML	MR	MT	MS	L	XL
D-01a	Cub Scouts	1957~±1959	Diamond shape. Wolf head has good detail. Snout is narrow between the eyes, wider at the bottom, raised and rounded. The distance between the eyes and the ears are narrow, with a raised area that has an indent in the center. The B & A of BSA are angled outward and curved in at the top inside of the letters "B" & "A". The ears are raised with no indent. Paw has the 4 toes spread apart at the top. A solid paw.	[ ]								
D-01b	Cub Scouts	±1959~±1972	Similar to 01a above except: The wolf head has more space between the ears and eyes. Snout is narrower. There is a narrow indent most of the length of the ears. There is a dimple in the paw.	[ ]				[ ]				
D-01c	Cub Scouts	±1959~±1972	Similar to 01b above except: There is a wider indent most of the length of the ears. There are three lines on the head between the ears and eyes.	[ ]								
D-01d	Cub Scouts	±1959~±1972	Similar to 01c above except: Face more squared at bottom.		[ ]		[ ]					
D-01e	Cub Scouts		Similar to 01d above except: Snout is smooth on the bottom portion.				[ ]					
D-01f	Cub Scouts	±1972~±1990	Similar to 01d above except: Lettering is thicker and flat on the top.					[ ]				
D-01g	Cub Scouts		Similar to 01d above except: Eyes have deep round socket.					[ ]				
D-01h	Cub Scouts		Wolf head is oval. Two pointed ears (similar to an inverted "V"). Toes are well spaded at the top. Eyes have 2 raised lines, pointed at the outside. Snout has 2 vertical parallel lines between the eyes, and raised (rounded) at the bottom. Thin toes.		[ ]							
D-01i	Cub Scouts	±1990~±1992	Similar to 01g above except: Face is more round, two lined between eyes are in the shape of a "V". Snout is flatter. Lettering is thinner at the top.							[ ]		
D-01j	Cub Scouts	±1993~2012	Mirror finish. Head is round and flat with no detail. Ears point outward with slight indent inside. Eyes are long and narrow, pointed at both ends and upward about 20° on the outside. Snout is flat and same width from top to bottom, slightly curved at the top and bottom. 3 lines angled 45° downward from snout and right eye to lower right side of head. 2 lines angled 80° downward to the left from bottom of eye to lower part of left side of head. The two left and right toes are parallel with the edge of the device and creating a wide space between the top portion of the 2 center toes. BSA is straight up and down.							[ ]		
D-01k	Cub Scouts		Similar to D-01f above except: Wolf head has more depth to face. There are 4 lines angled at 60° downward from bottom of both eyes to the lower portion of face.								[ ]	

[51] Prepared with assistance from George Crowl. Terry Grove assisted with the Distinguished Eagle device. This listing may be reproduced (NOT ELECTRONICALLY) for your personal use only. George Crowl has all the devices pictured on his web site: *http://www.crowl.org/George/* Please refer to his web site to see a scan of each device listed.

Snout is wider at the bottom than the top, with a raised area at the bottom of snout. The "B" and "A" of BSA are angled slightly inward at the top. Paw has one raised spot with 4 straight lines for the toes which are slightly wider at the top then bottom.

Nmbr	Insignia	Dates	Characteristics	S	M	MB	ML	MR	MT	MS	L	XL
D-01l	Cub Scouts	2012~2013	Similar to D-01g above except: Ears are above the face and not partly inside the face. There are 4 distinct whiskers on each side of snout angled at 45° downward from snout and lower portion of eyes to outside of face. The "B" and "S" of the BSA have a greater angle inward at the top. This device has 6 toes are straight lines, the 2 center toes, The 2 in the center are parallel and touching, while the 2 outer toes are parallel with the sides. The 2nd and 5th toe are toughing the center toes at the bottom and slight space at the top. Paw has one raised spot.								[ ]	
D-01m	Cub Scouts	2014~present	Similar to D01l above except: Face has more depth, left ear is off to the side more, more detail in the nose and forehead. There are four toes. Pad is shaped like a shield.								[ ]	

Nmbr	Insignia	Dates	Characteristics	S	M	MB	ML	MR	MT	MS	L	XL
D-02a	Boy Scouts	1957~±1959	Shape of Tenderfoot pin, fully cut, 13 stars (7 on the top row and 6 on the bottom row). In the lower portion of the shield there are 6 raised vertical lines creating 7 stripes in good detail. There is a bar separating the stars from the stripes below. Shield is wide. Beak is open and eye has a large opening. 2 stars (1 below each wing) pointing downward. 3 feathers over 5 feathers on each wing.	[ ]								
D-02b	Boy Scouts	±1959~	Similar to D-02a above except: Beak is closed. One row of 7 dots for stars (top) and a bar with 6 dots on it that separates the stars from the stripes. Shield is narrower. In the lower portion of the shield there are 4 vertical lines creating 5 strips. Narrow space between the 2nd, 3rd and 4th vertical lines, wide space both sides of the 1st vertical line. Wings have 2 feathers over 5 feathers.	[ ]								
D-02c	Boy Scouts		Similar to D-02b above except: The bar is slanted downward on the left. The bar has some raised bumps on it, none are clearly defined. Of the 4 vertical lines (creating stripes), the 1st is against the shield on the left side, 2nd line is in the center of the shield with the 3rd, and 4th line fairly evenly spaced. Eye has a triangular shape and extends to the center of the head.	[ ]								
D-02d	Boy Scouts		Similar to D-02c except: The eye is a circular depression. The 3rd vertical line is much closer to the 2nd line then the 4th line.	[ ]								
D-02e	Boy Scouts		Similar to D-02d above except: Top of shield offset to right. 3 vertical lines (creating stripes) that are fairly evenly spaced in the lower part of shield. Device has some fill-in between the tail and wing	[ ]								

area. Head is rounded at the top and is
more raised. Beak is noticeable.

Nmbr	Insignia	Dates	Characteristics	S	M	MB	ML	MR	MT	MS	L	XL
D-02f	Boy Scouts		Similar to D-02e above except: Shield has only 3 stars, and a bar with 6 slightly raised bumps on it. only 2 short vertical lines (not touching the bar or the shield). Major fill-in between the upper and lower portion of the FDL.	[ ]								
D-02g	Boy Scouts		Similar to D-02c above except: Shield is narrower and thicker at the top of the raised portion. Eye extends well into the beak.	[ ]								
D-02h	Boy Scouts	1969~1975	Similar to D-02d above except: Top of shied is wide and flat. There are 2 rows of stars 7 above 6. The second row replaces the horizontal bar. There are 3 wide flat vertical stripes, evenly spaced. The knees are thick, smooth and wide. Tail has 3 thick vertical lines for tail feathers.			[ ]						
D-02i	Boy Scouts	1975	Similar to D-02f above except: Top of shield is not as wide and is rounded at the top. Knees have minimal detail. The 3 vertical lines for the tail feathers are as thick and are rounded at the top. Shield is narrower.		[ ]							
D-02j	Boy Scouts		Similar to D-02f above except: There are no upper feathers in the wings. Fill-in complete between the upper and lower portion of the FDL. Raised oval between the shield, head, beak, and wing.						[ ]			
D-02k	Boy Scouts	1975~1980	Similar to D-02c above except: The top row of stars has 4 defined bumps, and then the remaining stars are all merged together. The second row of stars has 6 raised dots with no horizontal bar. 3 thick vertical lines with a space between the dots and the bars at the upper portion and touching the shield at the lower portion. 3 raised bars for tail feathers. Some fill-in between upper and lower extensions.							[ ]		
D-02l	Boy Scouts		Similar to D-02i above except: There are only 2 vertical bars in the shield. 1 in the center and the 2nd to the right of center.						[ ]			
D-02m	Boy Scouts	1980~1991	This device is re-designed. Shield is wide with 2 rows of bumps for stars, 7 over 6. Horizontal bar below stars. 6 vertical lines in lower portion of shield, evenly spaced. Wings have 2 rows of feathers, 5 inside feathers and 8 outside feathers. Stars outside of feathers are large, pointing down. Fill in, and area above the has a few small pebbles in it.								[ ]	[ ][ ][52]
D-02n	Boy Scouts	1980~1991	Similar to D-02m above except: Beak is smaller. Head is lower than and the neck is thicker. Area above the head is pebbled. Fill-in completely flat.		[ ]							
D-02o	Boy Scouts	2010~2011	This device is re-designed. Head is curved at the top from the beak to the head feathers. There is a dod for the eye. Wings have 2 rows of feathers, 5 inside feathers and 10 outside feathers. Shield has 2 rows of dots for stars, upper row has 5 and lower								[ ]	

---

[52] Two varieties, 1 is long from the center and the second is long from the bottom.

row has 4.   There are 5 evenly spaced stripes.

Nmbr	Insignia	Dates	Characteristics	S	M	MB	ML	MR	MT	MS	L	XL
D-02p	Boy Scouts	2011~2012	Top of head is angled like an inverted "V". Eye is long. Neck is angled slightly to the left. Shield is wider with 5 stars over 4 stars. Left wing has 2 distinct feathers on the outside and inside, the right wing has 3 distinct feathers on the outside with 1 on the inside, all other feathers are filled in. The bottom of the shield has 5 evenly spaced lines. Stars on FLD are right side up.								[ ][53]	
D-02q	Boy Scouts	2012~2013	Similar to D-02o above except: Eye is slightly longer. Shield has 3 rows of dots for stars. Top row has 1 dot, 2nd row has 5 dots and 3rd row has 4 dots.									
D-02r	Boy Scouts	2013~present	Similar to D-02o above except: Eye is longer. Wings have 3 over 5 feathers. Shield has 3 rows of dots for stars, top row has 7 dots, 2nd row has 9 dots, and 3rd row has 7 dots.								[ ][54]	

Nmbr	Insignia	Dates	Characteristics	S	M	MB	ML	MR	MT	MS	L	XL
D-03	Exploring CAW	1957 ~ 1958	Circular with compass points. FDL over compass, wings over FDL, and anchor on top.	[X]								

Nmbr	Insignia	Dates	Characteristics	S	M	MB	ML	MR	MT	MS	L	XL
D-04a	Commissioner	1957~	Circular with wreath around the outside edge. 1st class emblem. Rounded (not flat) surface. Space between the wreath and the top of the emblem. Top of emblem and bottom of knot does not exceed beyond the circle of the wreath. Thick neck on eagle. Eye in the center of the head. Dots for stars on the FDL. Shield has 5 stripes and no stars.	[ ]								
D-04b	Commissioner		Similar to D-04a above except: The top of the 1st class emblem and the bottom of the knot extend above and below the circle. Narrow shield, straight across at the top.	[ ]					[ ]			
D-04c	Commissioner		Similar to D-04b above except: Thinner neck.	[ ]	[ ]							
D-04d	Commissioner		Similar to D-04a above except: Not as raised in the center. Thin neck, raised outline touches on in the center of the neck. Upper portion of the shield curves up to a point in the top center.	[ ]								
D-04e	Commissioner		Similar to D-04d above except: Neck wide at the bottom and narrowing closes near the head (upside down "V" appearance). Top of shield is indented straight across. Extra dots on the bottom right of the FDL and upper right of the scroll.						[ ]			
D-04f	Commissioner		Similar to D-04e above except: Long thin neck. Shield comes to a point at the top center.		[ ]				[ ]			
D-04g	Commissioner		Almost flat design. There is a neck that widens at the bottom. Shield is taller.		[ ]							
D-04h	Commissioner		Similar to D-04g above except: Head is									[ ]

---

[53] Long from the top.
[54] Long from the top.

bent over and not defined.

Nmbr	Insignia	Dates	Characteristics	S	M	MB	ML	MR	MT	MS	L	XL
D-04i	Commissioner		Re-designed device. Round device with wreath and Tenderfoot emblem in center. Wings have 2 feathers over 5 feathers. Shield has 5 evenly spaced vertical stripes. Head upright with a thick neck and no eye. FDL does not touch the wreath. 2 stars on the FDL. 2 thick vertical bars at the bottom center of the wreath.							[ ]		
D-04j	Commissioner	2010~2011	Similar to D-04i above except: Eye in head. 3 feather over 5 feathers on the wing. Bars are not as thick on the bottom center of the wreath.								[ ]	[ ][55]
D-04k	Commissioner	2012~Present	Tenderfoot emblem is redesigned. There are 3 feathers over 4 feathers. Shield is wider with 3 vertical stripes. Rim of shield is thick. Head is thinner with an eye in the head. Neck thicker at bottom and narrowing at the top. 2 thin vertical bars at the bottom center of the wreath. Wreath is thicker than the other devices.							[ ]		

Nmbr	Insignia	Dates	Characteristics	S	M	MB	ML	MR	MT	MS	L	XL
D-05	Exploring Circle V	1958 ~ 1972	Universal Exploring emblem with 3 rings, V, and FDL – all gold.	[X]								

Nmbr	Insignia	Dates	Characteristics	S	M	MB	ML	MR	MT	MS	L	XL
D-06	Air Explorer	1959 ~ 1966	Shape of universal Air Scout/Explorer wings with FDL in center.	[X]								

Nmbr	Insignia	Dates	Characteristics	S	M	MB	ML	MR	MT	MS	L	XL
D-07a	Sea Explorer	1957~±1959	1st class emblem in front of anchor. Fully cut except the side of the FDL. Shield is only an outline Lettering well defined. No eye in head.	[ ]								
D-07b	Sea Explorer	±1959~1969	Similar to D-07a above except: Lettering is smaller and not well defined.		[ ][56]							
D-07c	Sea Explorer	1969~1990	Similar to D-07b above except: Area between top of FLD and top of anchor is filled in. Eye in head.							[ ]		
D-07d	Sea Explorer/Scouts	1990~2005	Similar to D-07c above except: Feathers in wings. Shield if solid and flat. Head is larger, no eye. Lettering is well defined. Fill-in between tip of scroll and tip of anchor.						[ ]	[ ]		
D-07e	Sea Scouts	2005~2014	Similar to D-07c above except: Head is much larger. Shield and tail filled in except 1 spot for a tail feather. Raised dots in place of lettering. No feathers.								[ ][57]	[ ][58]
D-07f	Sea Scouts	2014~present	Similar to D-07e above except: The back space to the left of the scroll is missing. The flat areas and the anchor are lightly pebbled.		[ ]							

Nmbr	Insignia	Dates	Characteristics	S	M	MB	ML	MR	MT	MS	L	XL
D-08	Distinguished Eagle	1969	**Approval Process** - These devices are not part of the listing. They are only lists to show the approval process of devices with precious metal.									

---

[55] Smooth with hook
[56] Stem is short from the center and a 2nd short stem from the top.
[57] One device is long and a second device is long with a hook at base of stem.
[58] Hook at base of stem.

Nmbr	Insignia	Dates	Characteristics	S	M	MB	ML	MR	MT	MS	L	XL
			1 Bronze (non-precious medal) device. Large beak pointing slightly upward. Defined neck feathers. Branches straight. Breast feathers are raised blotches on the breast.		[ ]							
			2 Similar to 1. above, except neck feathers are not as defined. Device is gold plated.		[ ]							
D-08a	Distinguished Eagle	1970 ~ 1978	14K gold, full breast feathers, medium length tail feathers, good detail in head, Beak pointed slightly upward to the left. Wing feathers are apparent and wing is curved. Talons are thick. Stamped 14Kr on back of tail. The "r" stands for Robbins.		[ ]							
D-08b	Distinguished Eagle	1970 ~ 1978	Similar to 08b above, except. beak is more pointed and neck is angled to the left. Stamped r14K on back of tail.		[ ]							
D-08c	Distinguished Eagle	1978 ~ 1979	Wings are not as full, with large space between wings and head. Head is tilted backward. Wings are not curved. Other features are similar to 08b above. Stamped 10K-GF on wing.		[ ]							
D-08d	Distinguished Eagle	1969 ~ 1970	Similar to the prototype, except the beak and top of head not as defined. Neck feathers are less defined and flat. Breast feathers are cuts into the breast. Gold plated. Branches have a slight arc. No hallmark.		[ ]							
D-08e	Distinguished Eagle	1979 ~ 1980	Similar to 08a above except. Head is more defined, beak is pointed upward. Neck feathers are more defined (4 long feathers). Wings are not curved. Space between neck and wings. Stamped S for Stange and GF for gold filled on back (facing to the right).		[ ]							
D-08f	Distinguished Eagle	1980 ~ 1985	Similar to 08e above, except fill in between head and wings.									
			1 Stamped S over G.F., facing upright.		[ ]							
			2 Stamped $ over G.F. facing upside down		[ ]							
			3 Stamped $ left of GF		[ ]							
			4 Stamped S over 1/10 10K								[ ]	
D-08g	Distinguished Eagle	1998 ~ 1999	Re-designed. Wings are wider and deeper. They extend further down the body, and very little space between neck/head and wings. Head above wings. Wing and body flat. BSA on center of device with S slightly higher than the B & A. Very Short and straight tail. Stamped Double S for Stange and 1/10 10K on back.								[ ]	
D-08h	Distinguished Eagle	1998 ~ 1999	Similar to D-08g above, except. Device is dull, top of BSA is wider. There are 4 branches with the ends merged together. Stamped .925 on back for sterling with gold plate.								[ ]	
D-08i	Distinguished Eagle	1999 ~ 2007	Wider space between head/neck and wings. Body of Eagle has depth. BSA on center of device. S is higher than B & A. Talons are thick. Slight arc to the branches talons are holding. Both ends of the branches are solid, and the lines do not extend to the end of the braches. Four defined feathers on the									

knees. Beak angles slightly downward. Eye is a raised dot. Neck feathers on the right side only. Very short curved tail.

Nmbr	Insignia	Dates	Characteristics	S	M	MB	ML	MR	MT	MS	L	XL
			1 Stamped CFJ on back.								[ ]	
			2 No hallmark								[ ]	
D-08j	Distinguished Eagle	2008	Dull device. Wings curve gradually to top of feet. Wings are fairly flat, slightly raised body. Tail is short and curved. Long talons with indent at in front of 2nd branch. Distinctive BSA that is curved. Stamped STER on back.									[ ]
D-08k	Distinguished Eagle	2009 ~ 2012	Shiny device. Stamped 10K on back of tail. Small spike at the bottom of device by Stem.									
			1 2010~2011 Stamped 🅂 left of 10K.									[ ]
			2 2011~2012 Stamped with a 🅂 over 10K.									[ ]
			3 2009~2010 Stamped 10K (small) on back of tail.									[ ]
			4 2010 Stamped large 10K on back tail.									[ ]
D-08l	Distinguished Eagle	2013 ~ present	Similar to D-08k above except: Slightly greater space between the back of the head and the wing. Neck feathers extend only 2/3rd the way from the top of the "S" and the eye. Eye is a round dot inset into the head. Stamped Large 10K on back tail.									[ ]
D-08m	Distinguished Eagle	2013 ~ present	Similar to D-08l above except: Beak and head are the same level with only a line separating them. Left foot, middle talon does not have a line through the center. That toe and the one to the right, have an indent between them higher than where the line is on the right toe. Stamped Large 10K on back tail.									[ ]
D-08n	Distinguished Eagle	2013 ~ present	Similar to D-08l above except: Eye is a dot with a long line to the left of the dot. Stamped Large 10K on back tail.									[ ]
Nmbr	Insignia	Dates	Characteristics	S	M	MB	ML	MR	MT	MS	L	XL
D-09a	Exploring Big E	1971~	Shape of Exploring Big E – Matte Finish.						[ ]			
D-09b	Exploring Big E	~1998	Shape of Exploring Big E – Mirror Finish.		[ ]				[ ]		[ ]	
D-09c	Exploring Big E	2004~2009	Shape of Exploring Big E – Semi-matte Finish.						[ ]			
D-09d	Exploring Big E	2009~2012	Similar to D-09b above except: Ridge of Big E is deeper.						[ ]			
D-09e	Exploring Big E	2010~present	Similar to D-09b above except: Background of Big E is pebbled.						[ ]			
Nmbr	Insignia	Dates	Characteristics	S	M	MB	ML	MR	MT	MS	L	XL
D-10a	Varsity Scouts	1985~±1993	The S overlaps the V at the top of the device. Bottom of the V is square. The top edges of the V & S are defined.							[ ]		
D-10b	Varsity Scouts	±1993~±2000	The S and V touch at the top and bottom of the device. (Card with old catalog number and new bar code).							[ ]		
D-10c	Varsity Scouts	±2000~2007	The S and V touch at the top of the device. Edges of the V follow the rim. The top edges of the V & S are curved.							[ ]		
D-10d	Varsity Scouts	2007~2009	There is a gap between the S and V. The top of the left leg of the V is curved. The top edges of the V & S are curved. Mirror							[ ]		

finish.

Nmbr	Insignia	Dates	Characteristics	S	M	MB	ML	MR	MT	MS	L	XL
D-10e	Varsity Scouts	2009~2012	There is a gap between the S and V. The top of the left leg of the V is curved. The top edges of the V & S are defined. This device is dull with sharp detail.		[ ]							
D-10f	Varsity Scouts	2012~present	The S and V are toughing. The top of the left leg of the V is curved. The top edges of the V & S are defined. Notch in lower portion of left leg.		[ ]							

Nmbr	Insignia	Dates	Characteristics	S	M	MB	ML	MR	MT	MS	L	XL
D-11a	Webelos	1989~1995	Diamond with raised rim. Universal Webelos emblem inside slightly raised.							[ ]		
D-11b	Webelos	1995~2011	Diamond with raised rim. Universal Webelos emblem inside and noticeably raised edges curved at top.		[ ]						[ ]	
D-11c	Webelos	2011~present	Similar to D-11b above except: Top of diamond is flat and wide.								[ ]	

Nmbr	Insignia	Dates	Characteristics	S	M	MB	ML	MR	MT	MS	L	XL
D-12a	District Committee	1993	Circular, raised rim with 1st class emblem in center. Shield has 13 stars and 5 vertical stripes. Rim of the shield is narrow.							[ ]		
D-12b	District Committee	1993~2008	Re-designed device. Circular, raised rim with FDL in center. Wings of Eagle have 3 short upper feathers and 5 long lower feathers per wing. Thick neck on eagle. Shield has 5 stripes.		[ ]					[ ]		
D-12c	District Committee	2008~2013	Similar to D-12b above except: Wings of Eagle have 3 upper feathers and 4 lower feathers per wing. Neck of the eagle is thinner with a larger eye on the head. Shield has a thick rim. Tail feathers spread out.								[ ]	
D-12d	District Committee	2013~present	Similar to D-12c above, except: Rim is shallow. Top of head is almost straight across with the eye going almost to the top of the head. Shield has 4 dots for stars following the contour of the top of the shield. Each wing has 1 row of 4 feathers.								[ ]	

Nmbr	Insignia	Dates	Characteristics	S	M	MB	ML	MR	MT	MS	L	XL
D-13a	Venturing	1998~2003	Top of diamond has raised mountains, straight line (depression) across the middle. Bottom has a V offset to the right. Mirror finish on raised area. Depressions in the V and sky are matte finish.							[ ]		
D-13b	Venturing	2003~2008	Similar to D-13a above except: Left mountain peak is shallow and cut into.							[ ]	[ ]	
D-13c	Venturing	2008~2013	Similar to D-12b above except: Light pebbling.								[ ]	
D-13d	Venturing	2013~present	Re-designed upper area of the device. Mountains are lower and peaks are pointed. All 3 recessed areas are pebbled.								[ ]	

Nmbr	Insignia	Dates	Characteristics	S	M	MB	ML	MR	MT	MS	L	XL
D-14a	1910 Society	2000~2005	Circular with triangle – point down, FDL extending above triangle. There are 2 horizontal bars behind top of FDL. Wreath outside bottom half. Ribbon below FDL with 1910 Society on it. Wreath around outside extending up to just below the top of the triangle. Thick lettering 9 & 0 are mostly filled in.							[ ]		

Nmbr	Insignia	Dates	Characteristics	S	M	MB	ML	MR	MT	MS	L	XL
D-14b	1910 Society	2005~2010	Similar to D-14a above except: Lettering 9 & 0 are not filled in and not as thick.							[ ]		
D-14c	1910 Society	2000~2011	Similar to D-14b above except: Lettering is thinner and very clear.							[ ]		

Nmbr	Insignia	Dates	Characteristics	S	M	MB	ML	MR	MT	MS	L	XL
D-15a	Founder's Circle	2000~2005	Round with compass having 4 main points extending outside the rim & 8 smaller points extending to the edge of the circle. Larger circle inside has the words Founders Circle, and a smaller circle has the FDL inside. First device made in silver. Lettering is clear and well defined.	[ ]								
D-15b	Founder's Circle	2005~2010	Similar to D-15a above except: Lettering is not as clear. Detail of the FDL is not as clear.							[ ]		
D-15c	Founder's Circle	2000~2011	Similar to D-15b above except: Lettering is difficult to read.							[ ]		

Nmbr	Insignia	Dates	Characteristics	S	M	MB	ML	MR	MT	MS	L	XL
D-16	Philmont Training Center	2009~present	Rectangular device. Yellow center with raised PTC in center. Center of letters are colored Red, with gold on the outer edge of letters and raised outer edge of device. Small spike on back to prevent device from turning on knot.								[ ]	

Nmbr	Insignia	Dates	Characteristics	S	M	MB	ML	MR	MT	MS	L	XL
D-17a	Adams NES Service Project of the Year Award - Council	2011	Bronze pin with an Eagle with wings spread upwards, head down to left, talons below head to left, "BSA" over tail. Centered between the main portion of the wings is a "V" with 6 half rings at top and a flame above the half rings. Body feathers start slightly in front of the back wing feathers, angling down towards the top center of the S of BSA. then angle (at approximately 90°) forward towards the top left of the B of BSA. Some feathering is missing on the leg over the S of BSA. There are 8 tail feathers between the B and lower right end of the A of BSA. One of the feathers is very slightly raised. Top talon is thin, middle one is thick while the bottom talon is a medium thickness. Hallmark with EB in a circle on the back.								[ ]	
D-17b	Adams NES Service Project of the Year Award - Council	2012	Similar to D-17a above, except: The 5th tail feather from the left is missing. Body feathering starts further back and does not angle as far forward. Feathering over the leg is not as noticeable.							[ ]		
D-17c	Adams NES Service Project of the Year Award - Council	2013	Similar to D-17a above, except: The 5th tail feather is present, with a larger space between the 4th and 5th feather than between the other feathers.							[ ]		
D-17d	Adams NES Service Project of the Year Award - Council	2014	Similar to D-17a above, except: The color of the device is lighter. Body feathering comes forward near the eye. The mouth angles downward. Leg feathering is missing in an inverted "V" shape over the S of BSA.							[ ]		

Nmbr	Insignia	Dates	Characteristics	S	M	MB	ML	MR	MT	MS	L	XL
D-18a	Adams NES Service Project of the Year Award - Regional	2011~2012	Similar to D-17a above, except: Device is Gold instead of bronze. Talons are thinner than the D-17 Body feathering starts slightly in front of the back feathers angling toward the top of the leg, then after 1/4 of the body, angles towards the top of the B in BSA. The feathering on the leg from the S in BSA upward to the top of the leg that has an hourglass shape without any feathering. The top of that is straight across. Hallmark has EB inside an oval and 10k to the right.								[ ]	
D-18b	Adams NES Service Project of the Year Award - Regional	2013~present	Similar to D-18a above, except: Feathering on the body is smaller. The neck and body feathers are smaller and more defined. Area above the S of BSA and the top of the leg appears more of a rectangular solid with some feathering near the top of the S. Hallmark has an oval with EB inside an oval above 10k.								[ ]	
D-18c	Adams NES Service Project of the Year Award - Regional	2014	Similar to D-18a above, except: The feathering on the body is larger and more defined. The area above the S of BSA on the leg has a heart shaped area (clockwise laying sideways) with no feathering. Hallmark on back with EB inside circle on left wing tip and 10K on right wing tip as viewed from the back.								[ ]	

Nmbr	Insignia	Dates	Characteristics	S	M	MB	ML	MR	MT	MS	L	XL
D-19a	Adams NES Service Project of the Year Award - National	2011~2012	Similar to D-17a above, except: Silver pin with an Eagle with wings spread upwards, head down to left, talons below head to left, "BSA" over tail. BSA is thick and flat. Centered between the main portion of the wings is a "V" with 6 half rings at top and a flame above the half rings. Feathering on body is not distinct. Hallmark has an oval with EB inside and SS to the right.								[ ]	
D-19b	Adams NES Service Project of the Year Award - National	2013	Similar to D-19a above, except: The neck and body feathers are both longer and smaller, also more defined. BSA is thinner and rounded. Area on leg above the S of BSA to the top of the leg has no feathering in a wide hourglass shape with a straight line at the top of that area. Hallmark has an oval with EB inside above SS.								[ ]	
D-19c	Adams NES Service Project of the Year Award - National	2014	Similar to D-19a above, except: Feathering on body is larger. Area on leg above the S of BSA to the top of the leg has no feathering in a hourglass shape with a straight line at the top of that area. Hallmark, on back, has an EB inside an oval on the left wing top and SS on the right wing tip as view from the back.								[ ]	

Nmbr	Insignia	Dates	Characteristics	S	M	MB	ML	MR	MT	MS	L	XL
D-20a	NOESA	2011~2012	Round silver pin with ribbon effect with the 2 ends near the top. Eagle with wings stretched out in flying position in front of ribbon. Wings exceed the diameter of the device. Left wing is higher than the right wing. Head slightly to left. NOESA across the bottom of the device. A round handle extending down from the circle.								[ ]	

Nmbr	Insignia	Dates	Characteristics	S	M	MB	ML	MR	MT	MS	L	XL
D-20b	NOESA	2012~present	Device re-designed. Round device with an inner circle forming a wide band around the outside. An eagle with wings stretched out and upwards, talons and tail down. Head to the right. "BSA" inside the band at the top. "NOESA" in the band at the bottom of the device. Antique silver.								[ ]	

Nmbr	Insignia	Dates	Characteristics	S	M	MB	ML	MR	MT	MS	L	XL
D-21	OA Legacy Fellowship	2011~present	Dull copper arrowhead with indents.								[ ]	

Nmbr	Insignia	Dates	Characteristics	S	M	MB	ML	MR	MT	MS	L	XL
D-22	Tiger Cub Den Leader	2012~present	Shinny diamond device with a tiger head centered from left to right at the top of the device. The head is about half the size of the device. FDL at the bottom center. The lettering "Tiger Cub" is hard to read between the head and FDL.								[ ][59]	

Nmbr	Insignia	Dates	Characteristics	S	M	MB	ML	MR	MT	MS	L	XL
D-23	NESA Legacy Society	2013~present	The bottom 3/5th of a circular shield with "National Eagle Scout Association". Below the circle is a solid rectangular bar. The center of the circular shield is filled in with 2 raised vertical lines. Above that is an eagle.								[ ]	

Abbreviations

Column Headings (Listed Alphabetically)

Characteristics	Description of device	ME	Medium post attached on the side of the device
Dates	Dates of issue	MS	Medium – thick, smooth post – attached at center of device.
Insignia	Name of device	MT	Medium post attached at top of device
L	Long post	Nmbr	Number and letter for device
LB	Long post from bottom of device	S	Short post
M	Medium post attached at center of device - notched	XL	Extra long post
MB	Medium post attached at the bottom of the device		

Disclaimer

The device listing is as complete as my research has been able to document. I am aware that it may not be complete and welcome additional information. Please contact me if you have an device that is different than those listed.

To see a scan of each device listed in the Listing of Knot Device Issues (D-List), go to web site: *http://www.crowl.org/George/* Reference: Varieties of Official BSA Square Knots, Knot Devices.

---

[59] There are 2 variations: 1 is a long stem & the second is a long stem from the bottom.

Rearrangement of devices from the 6th Edition

To align the devices based on when they were manufactured, a rearrangement of the order was accomplished for some of the named devices. All devices were not rearranged. The devices that were changed are listed below with the changes.

Cub Scout Device

Device	From	Device	From	Device	From	Device	From	Device	From
D-01a	Added	D-01b	D-01a	D-01c	D-01a	D-01d	D-01b	D-01e	D-01c
D-01f	Added	D-01g	D-01d	D-01h	Added	D-01i	Added	D-01j	Added
D-01k	Added	D-01l	Added	D-01m	Added				

Boy Scout Device

Device	From	Device	From	Device	From	Device	From	Device	From
D-02a	Added	D-02b	D-02a	D-02c	Added	D-02d	Added	D-02e	D-02b
D-02f	Added	D-02g	D-02c	D-02h	Added	D-02i	D-02d	D-02j	D-02e
D-02k	Added	D-02l	D-02f	D-02m	Added	D-02n	Added	D-02o	Added
D-02p	Added	D-02q	Added	D-02r	Added				

Commissioner Device

Device	From	Device	From	Device	From	Device	From	Device	From
D-04a	D-04a	D-04b	D-04b	D-04c	Added	D-04d	D-04c	D-04e	D-04d
D-04f	Added	D-04g	D-04e	D-04h	Added	D-04i	D-04f	D-04j	Added
D-04k	Added								

Sea Scout Device

Device	From	Device	From	Device	From	Device	From	Device	From
D-07a	Added	D-07b	D-07a	D-07 c	D-07b	D-04d	D-07c	D-07e	Added

Distinguished Eagle Device

Device	From	Device	From	Device	From	Device	From	Device	From
D-08a	D-08a	D-08b	Added	D-08c	Added	D-08d	Added	D-08e	D-08b
D-08f1	D-08c1	D-08f2	Added	D-08f3	D-08c2	D-08f4	D-08c3	D-08g	D-08d
D-08h	Added	D-08i1	D-08e	D-08i2	Added	D-08j	D-08f	D-08k1	Added
D-08k2	Added	D-08k3	Added	D-08k4	D-08g	D-08l	Added	D-08m	Added
D-08n	Added								

Listing of Eagle Palms[60]

Number	Palm	Type	Back Information	SL	CL1	CL2	CL3	SS	MS	LS	MISC
EP-1a	Bronze	I	Gold Spin lock	[ ]							SL 13 mm
EP-1b	Bronze	II									
			1 Plain back	[ ]		[ ]					Sil SL 13 mm
			2 Raised "Genuine Bronze"	[ ]							SL 13 mm
			3 Stamped "Sterling"				[ ]				
EP-1c	Bronze	III									
			1 Plain back				[ ]				
			2 Raised "Genuine Bronze"	[ ]							Gold SL 15 mm SL 13 mm
			3 Raised "Sterling"			[ ]					
EP-1d	Bronze	IV									
			1 Plain Back	[ ]							SL 13 mm
			2 Raised "Genuine Bronze"	[ ]							SL 13 mm SL 13 mm, Sil Pin
			3 Raised "Sterling"			[ ]					
EP-1e	Bronze	V		[ ]							SL 13 mm
			1 Plain Back						[ ]		
			2 Raised "Genuine Bronze"	[ ]							SL 13 mm Sil SL 13 mm
EP-1f	Bronze	VI									
			1 Raised "Genuine Bronze"	[ ]							SL 13 mm
			2 Stamped "Genuine Bronze"	[ ]							Sil SL 13 mm
			3 Raised "Sterling"			[ ]					
EP-1g	Bronze	VII									
			1 Plain Back				[ ]				
			2 Raised "Genuine Bronze"	[ ]							SL 13 mm
EP-1h	Bronze	VIII									
			1 Plain Back			[ ]					
			2 Raised "Genuine Bronze"	[ ]		[ ]					Sil SL 13 mm SL 13 mm
EP-1i	Bronze	IX				[ ]	[ ]				
EP-1j	Bronze	X									
			1 Plain Back				[ ]				
			2 Raised "Genuine Bronze"				[ ]				
			3 Silver Stem							[ ]	
EP-1k	Bronze	XII	Silver Stem							[ ]	
EP-1l	Bronze	XIII							[ ]	[ ]	
EP-1m	Bronze	XIV	Silver Stem						[ ]		
EP-1n	Bronze	XV							[ ]		
EP-1o	Bronze	XVI						[ ]			
EP-1p	Bronze	XVIII							[ ]	[ ]	
EP-1q	Bronze	XXII							[ ]	[ ]	
EP-1r	Bronze	XXIII								[ ]	
EP-1s	Bronze	XXIV								[ ]	

---

[60] Prepared with assistance from Dr. Terry Grove. This listing may be reproduced (NOT ELECTRONICALLY) for your personal use only.

Number	Palm	Type	Back Information	SL	CL1	CL2	CL3	SS	MS	LS	MISC
EP-2a	Gold	I	Gold Spin lock	[ ]							SL 13 mm
EP-2b	Gold	II	Stamped "STERLING" on back			[ ]					
EP-2c	Gold	IV									
			1 Plain back	[ ]							SL 13 mm SL 15 mm
			2 Raised "Genuine Bronze"	[ ]	[ ]						SL 13 mm
			3 Raised "Sterling"				[ ]				
EP-2d	Gold	V		[ ]							SL 12 mm
EP-2e	Gold	VI								[ ]	
EP-2f	Gold	VII		[ ]							SL 15 mm
EP-2g	Gold	VIII		[ ]		[ ]					Sil SL 13 mm
EP-2h	Gold	X				[ ]		[ ]			
EP-2i	Gold	XI						[ ]			
EP-2j	Gold	XII						[ ]	[ ]		
EP-2k	Gold	XV									
			1 Gold Stem						[ ]		
			2 Silver Stem						[ ]		
EP-2l	Gold	XVI							[ ]		
EP-2m	Gold	XVII							[ ]		
EP-2n	Gold	XVIII							[ ]	[ ]	
EP-2o	Gold	XX								[ ]	
EP-2p	Gold	XXII							[ ]		
EP-2q	Gold	XXIII									
			1 Gold Stem							[ ]	
			2 Silver Stem							[ ]	
EP-2r	Gold	XXIV								[ ]	

Number	Palm	Type	Back Information	SL	CL1	CL2	CL3	SS	MS	LS	MISC
EP-3a	Silver	I	Raised "STERLING" on back	[ ]							SL 13 mm SL 14 mm
EP-3b	Silver	II	Stamped "TOP" on back			[ ]					
EP-3c	Silver	IV				[ ]					
EP-3d	Silver	V		[ ]							SL 12 mm SL 13 mm
EP-3e	Silver	VI		[ ]							SL 13 mm
EP-3f	Silver	VII									
			1 Plain back			[ ]					
			2 Stamped "STERLING TOP" on back	[ ]							SL 15 mm
EP-3g	Silver	VIII	Stamped "TOP" on back			[ ]					
EP-3h	Silver	IX								[ ]	
EP-3i	Silver	X						[ ]			
EP-3j	Silver	XI						[ ]			Dull
EP-3k	Silver	XII								[ ]	
EP-3l	Silver	XIII							[ ]		
EP-3m	Silver	XVI							[ ]		
EP-3n	Silver	XVIII							[ ]	[ ]	
EP-3o	Silver	XIX							[ ]		
EP-3p	Silver	XXI							[ ]		
EP-3q	Silver	XXII								[ ]	
EP-3r	Silver	XXIII								[ ]	
EP-3s	Silver	XXIV								[ ]	

Disclaimer

The Eagle Palm listing is as complete as my research has been able to document. I am aware that it may not be complete and welcome additional information. Please contact me if you have an Eagle Palm that is different than those listed/pictured.

Key Code

Number	Number assigned by color of palm	**Palm**	Color of Eagle Palm
Back Information	Anything stamped or raised on back.	**SL**	Spin Lock
CL1	Crude Lock - 13 mm long by 4 mm high	**CL2**	Crude Lock - 15 mm long by 5 mm high
CL3	Crude Lock - 16 mm long by 5 mm high	**SS**	Short Stem - Approximately 4 mm long
MS	Medium stem - Approximately 6 mm long	**LS**	Medium stem - Approximately 8 mm long
Misc	Miscellaneous information		

Types of Eagle Palms

Type I

Palm has a slight "S" curve from tip to quill. Spines start from approximately the same point on the quill except those at the tip which are offset. Quill is cut at a 60° angle from upper left to lower right and angled from front to back. There is a dimple in the cut of the quill.

Type II

Palm is redesigned so the quill has very little curvature. The spines at the tip, spine next to the tip, and the spine end have the same starting point, all others are offset. Quill is cut at a 45° angle from upper left to lower right and angled from front to back. There is a dimple between the side and end of the quill.

Type III

Similar to Type II except dimple is on the end of the quill.

Type IV

Similar to Type II except the end of the quill has the dimple on the side of the quill. The end of the quill is cut straight back. The end is cut at a 45° angle.

Type V

Similar Type IV above except: The end of the quill is cut at a 45° angle from front left to back right so the end is visable.

Type VI

Similar to Type V, except the cut on the quill is at a 60° angle and the quill is cut from front to back so the end is not visable.

117

Type VII

Tip similar to Type II. Quill has a dimple on the side and the quill cut straight back from the front.

Type VIII

Similar to Type VI except the cut is angled from the front right to the back left.

Type IX

Similar to Type II except the cut at the end of the stem is at a 30° angle. Spines at the tip are closer together at the tip.

Type X

Similar to Type IX except the quill is quill is cut at a 45° angle.

Type XI

Tip similar to Type VIII above. Dimple on side with the end of quill cut downward at a 60° angle and angled backward from the front.

Type XII

Similar to Type VII except the dimple is an outlined mark, and not a full dimple. The quill is cut at a 60° angle.

Type XIII

Palm is flatter then the others on the top. The quill is thicker at the end with the quill cut at a 60° angle from upper left to lower right and angled from front to back. There is no dimple.

Type XIV

Similar to Type XI except quill is cut straight back.

Type XV

Similar to XI above except: Stem is cut at an angle from front right to back left.

Type XVI

Similar to XV except: Face of palm is flatter and thicker.

Type XVII

Similar to Type VII except the quill is not as long, and narrow at the end. The end of the quill is cut from upper right to lower left (with a slight angle from front to back) at a 90° angle. Palm is flatter than previous.

Type XVIII

Similar to Type XVI except the spines are not as flat. Quill is cut at a 45° angle from top left to bottom right with the bottom tip angled back to the front. The quill is also cut straight back.

Type XIX

Similar to Type XVI except the palm is not as flat, the bottom stem on the tip is not as long, and the quill is angled forward at the end.

Type XX

Similar to Type VI except the quill is not as thick at the end. The end of the quill is cut at a 45° angle, There is a second cut verticlly from the top of the cut to the bottom extending to the lower tip of the quil.

Type XXI

This palm has more of an "S" curve then the previous types except Type I. Much flatter than the others. Quill is cut at a 90° angle from upper left to lower right, and straight back from front to back.

Type XXII

Palm resembles the shape of types VIII through XIII. The back of the palm has the general shape. The top has a detailed image of the palm. The upper portion has a double image.

Type XXIII

XXIV

Similar to Type XIII except the right upper portion of the quill is cut down, then horizontal to the end of the quill. The face of the spines are flatter and thicker.

Similar to Type XVII except there is a retangular dimple angled from lower left to upper right near the end of the quill.

Bibliography

Uniforms, Badges and Insignia, Boy Scouts of America, 1933
The Scout Executive, Vol. XIV, No. 9, November 1933
The Scout Executive, Vol. XV, No. 10, Boy Scouts of America, November 1934
The Scout Administrator, Vol. I, No. 9, October 1935
The Scout Administrator, Vol. III, No. 2, November 1937
The Local Council Exchange - Vol. 1, No. 3, November 1938
The Local Council Exchange - Vol. 2, No. 5, November 1939
The Local Council Exchange - Vol. 4, No. 2, May 1941
The Scout Executive, Vol. 12, No. 7, Boy Scouts of America, October 1947
Price List, Official Boy Scout Uniforms and Equipment, April 1, 1944
Price List, Official Boy Scout Uniforms and Equipment, January 15, 1945
Price List, Official Boy Scout Uniforms and Equipment, January 1, 1947
Official Uniforms and Equipment of the Boy Scouts of America, March 1951
Official Uniforms and Equipment of the Boy Scouts of America, June 1, 1951
Official Uniforms and Equipment of the Boy Scouts of America, January 1, 1953
Official Uniforms and Equipment of the Boy Scouts of America, June 1954
Official Uniforms and Equipment of the Boy Scouts of America, March 1, 1955
Official Uniforms and Equipment of the Boy Scouts of America, January 1, 1956
Official Uniforms and Equipment of the Boy Scouts of America, April 1, 1957
Official Uniforms and Equipment of the Boy Scouts of America, September 1, 1957
Official Uniforms and Equipment of the Boy Scouts of America, March 1, 1958
Official Uniforms and Equipment of the Boy Scouts of America, November 1, 1958
Official Uniforms and Equipment of the Boy Scouts of America, March 1, 1961
Official Uniforms and Equipment of the Boy Scouts of America, January 1, 1962
Official Uniforms and Equipment of the Boy Scouts of America, September 1, 1962
Official Uniforms and Equipment of the Boy Scouts of America, March 1, 1963
Official Uniforms and Equipment of the Boy Scouts of America, March 1, 1965
Official Uniforms and Equipment of the Boy Scouts of America, September 1, 1966
Official Uniforms and Equipment of the Boy Scouts of America, March 1, 1968
Official Uniforms and Equipment of the Boy Scouts of America, January 1, 1969
Official Uniforms and Equipment of the Boy Scouts of America, January 1, 1970
Official Uniforms and Equipment of the Boy Scouts of America, March 1, 1970
Official Uniforms and Equipment of the Boy Scouts of America, January 1, 1971
Official Uniforms and Equipment of the Boy Scouts of America, March 1, 1971
Official Uniforms and Equipment of the Boy Scouts of America, March 1, 1972
Official Uniforms and Equipment of the Boy Scouts of America, September 1, 1972
Official Uniforms and Equipment of the Boy Scouts of America, March 1, 1973
Official Uniforms and Equipment of the Boy Scouts of America, September 1973
Official Uniforms and Equipment of the Boy Scouts of America, March 1974
Official Uniforms and Equipment of the Boy Scouts of America, March 1975
Official Uniforms and Equipment of the Boy Scouts of America, August 1975
Official Uniforms and Equipment of the Boy Scouts of America, March 1976
Official Uniforms and Insignia, Boy Scouts of America, Cub Scouting, April 1953
Official Uniforms and Insignia, Boy Scouts of America, Boy Scouting, April 1953
Official Uniforms and Insignia, Boy Scouts of America, Exploring, April 1953
Official Uniforms and Insignia, Boy Scouts of America, Boy Scouting, Mar 1954
Official Uniforms and Insignia, Boy Scouts of America, Cub Scouting, September 1, 1955
Official Uniforms and Insignia, Boy Scouts of America, Boy Scouting, September 1, 1955

Official Uniforms and Insignia, Boy Scouts of America, Exploring, September 1, 1955
Official Uniforms and Insignia, Boy Scouts of America, Boy Scouting, October 1956
Official Uniforms and Insignia, Boy Scouts of America, Boy Scouting, November 1957
Official Uniforms and Insignia, Boy Scouts of America, Boy Scouting, January 1959
Official Uniforms and Insignia, Boy Scouts of America, Cub Scouting, September 1959
Official Uniforms and Insignia, Boy Scouts of America, Boy Scouting, April 1960
Official Uniforms and Insignia, Boy Scouts of America, Cub Scouting, January 1961
Official Uniforms and Insignia, Boy Scouts of America, Boy Scouting, January 1962
Official Uniforms and Insignia, Boy Scouts of America, Cub Scouting, December 1962
Official Uniforms and Insignia, Boy Scouts of America, Boy Scouting, December 1962
Official Uniforms and Insignia, Boy Scouts of America, Boy Scouting, January 1966
Official Uniforms and Insignia, Boy Scouts of America, Boy Scouting, August 1966
Official Uniforms and Insignia, Boy Scouts of America, Boy Scouting, January 1967
Official Uniforms and Insignia, Boy Scouts of America, September 1967
Official Uniforms and Insignia, Boy Scouts of America, January 1969
Official Uniforms and Insignia, Boy Scouts of America, May 1973
Insignia Control Guide, Boy Scouts of America, January 1978
Insignia Control Guide, Boy Scouts of America, May 1978
Insignia Control Guide, Boy Scouts of America, January 1979
Insignia Control Guide, Boy Scouts of America, October 1980
Insignia Control Guide, Boy Scouts of America, February 1982
Insignia Control Guide, Boy Scouts of America, July 1982
Insignia Control Guide, Boy Scouts of America, December 1982
Insignia Control Guide, Boy Scouts of America, October 1983
Insignia Control Guide, Boy Scouts of America, 1986 B
Insignia Control Guide, Boy Scouts of America, 1986 Revision
Insignia Control Guide, Boy Scouts of America, 1986 Second Printing
Insignia Guide, Boy Scouts of America, 1989
Insignia Guide, Boy Scouts of America, 1990
Insignia Guide, Boy Scouts of America, 1991
Insignia Guide, Boy Scouts of America, 1993
Insignia Guide, Boy Scouts of America, 1995
Insignia Guide, Boy Scouts of America, 1996
Insignia Guide, Boy Scouts of America, 1997
Insignia Guide, Boy Scouts of America, 1998
Insignia Guide, Boy Scouts of America, 1999
Insignia Guide, Boy Scouts of America, 2000
Insignia Guide, Boy Scouts of America, 2002
Insignia Guide, Boy Scouts of America, 2003-2005
Insignia Guide, Boy Scouts of America, 2005
Insignia Guide, Boy Scouts of America, 2006
Insignia Guide, Boy Scouts of America, #33066, 2007
Insignia Guide, Boy Scouts of America, #33066, 2008
Guide to Awards and Insignia, 2012
Leadership Training Committee Guide, Boy Scouts of America, #34169F, 2003
Leadership Training Committee Guide, Boy Scouts of America, #34169, 2008
National Recognition of Local Council Endowment Support, Boy Scouts of America, Publication 35-555A
Prospeak, Boy Scouts of America, Vol. 19, No. 2, February 2005
Scouting Magazine, Boy Scouts of America, February 1940

Scouting Magazine, Boy Scouts of America, March 1946
Scouting Magazine, Boy Scouts of America, October 1956
Scouting Magazine, Boy Scouts of America, September 1977
Scouting Magazine, Boy Scouts of America, March-April 1978
Scouting Magazine, Boy Scouts of America, September 1979
Scouting Magazine, Boy Scouts of America, November-December 1979
Scouting Magazine, Boy Scouts of America, May-June 1980
Scouting Magazine, Boy Scouts of America, September 1980
Scouting Magazine, Boy Scouts of America, October 1982
Scouting Magazine, Boy Scouts of America, September 1983
Scouting Magazine, Boy Scouts of America, May-June 1985
Scouting Magazine, Boy Scouts of America, January-February 1987
Scouting Magazine, Boy Scouts of America, September 1987
Scouting Magazine, Boy Scouts of America, November-December 1987
Scouting Magazine, Boy Scouts of America, September 1988
Scouting Magazine, Boy Scouts of America, October 1989
Scouting Magazine, Boy Scouts of America, November-December 1989
Scouting Magazine, Boy Scouts of America, September 1991
Scouting Magazine, Boy Scouts of America, October 1992
Scouting Magazine, Boy Scouts of America, September 1997
Scouting Magazine, Boy Scouts of America, September 2000
Scouting Magazine, Boy Scouts of America, November-December 2000
Scouting Magazine, Boy Scouts of America, January-February 2005
Scouting Magazine, Boy Scouts of America, January-February 2009
BSA flier #13-083, 2006 printing
BSA flies # 532-555, 2009 printing
www.scouting.org, Boy Scouts of America web site
www.scouting.org/training/adult.aspx, Boy Scouts of America web site for training and training awards
www.scouting.org/filestore/pdf/Major_Gifts_Recognition_brochure.pdf, Major Gifts Recognition
www.scouting.org/filestore/training/pdf/Sea_Scout_Skippers_Key.pdf, Skippers Key Training
    requirements, January 1, 2014 Printing
www.scouting.org/filestore/training/pdf/Sea_Scout_Adult_Training_Award.pdf, Scouter's Training
    Award requirements for Sea Scout Leaders, January 1, 2014 Printing
www.scouting.org/filestore/training/pdf/districtcommscouterstrainingawd.pdf, District Committee
    Scouter's Training Award progress record
www.scouting.org/filestore/training/pdf/districtcommittekey.pdf, District Committee Key progress
    record
Book "100 Years of the Eagle Scout Award" by Dr. Terry Grove, Available for sale at
    www.groveagle.com
Publication 22-721, International Scouter's Award, 2002 Printing
Publication 511-052, Den Leader Training Award progress record, 2012 Printing
Publication 511-053, Cubmaster Key progress record, 2012 Printing
Publication 511-054, Scoutmaster's Key requirements, 2012 Printing
Publication 511-055, Coach's Key progress record, 2012 Printing
Publication 511-056, Advisor's Key progress record, 2012 Printing
Publication 511-057, Scouter's Training Award for Cub Scouting progress record, 2012 Printing
Publication 511-058, Scouter's Training Award for Boy Scouting requirements, 2012 Printing
Publication 511-059, Scouter's Training Award for Varsity Scouting requirements, 2012 Printing
Publication 511-060, Venturing Training Award requirements, 2012 Printing

53557923R00075

Made in the USA
Columbia, SC
17 March 2019